Spiritual Warfare:

Christians, Demonization and Deliverance

By Dr. Karl I. Payne

Karl Payne presents the Biblical and practical aspects of the reality of spiritual warfare in a clear and simple fashion. His Biblical and theological orientation and his years of experience in front line activity are reflected throughout this book. He boldly presents a solid and reasonable challenge to incorporate a Biblical worldview regarding our battle with demonic powers. All those concerned with promoting Biblical discipleship should profit from his years of concerned and studied involvement in this ministry.

—C. Fred Dickason, Th.D.
Professor Emeritus of Theology,
Moody Bible Institute

Karl Payne's desire to make a difference in the lives of others permeates everything he does. This is a must read for every artist, worship leader, musician, theologian and lay person. Here's a practical handbook on dealing with spiritual warfare.

—Dr. Stephen Michael Newby
Seattle Pacific University
Director of University Ministries and Worship
Director of worship for Promise Keepers USA

As I read this book, four important words came to mind: graphic, practical, balanced and Biblical. Dr. Payne's style grabs your attention with his graphic way of sharing facts; his practical insights help identify needs; his gracious words toward critics show loving balance; and his careful attention to Biblical truth commands respect. This book is a must read! "It is for freedom that Christ has set us free" (Galatians 5:1a). Karl Payne's book will help believers walk in their freedom.

—Dr. Mark I. Bubeck
President Emeritus,
Deeper Walk International.

Dr. Karl I. Payne has issued a provocative, Biblically based challenge for all Christians, regardless of their denominational, ecclesiastical or theological loyalties, to consider or reconsider the subject of spiritual warfare in general, and demonic warfare specifically.

He writes with the passion of a prophet, the urgency of an exhorter, the care and concern of a shepherd, the courage of an apologist and the clarity and transferability of a discipleship trainer. The tone and tenor of this book are neither patronizing nor pompous; it is as practical as it is pragmatic.

I am pleased to have the opportunity to recommend the reading and study of this insightful and timely book to Christians who desire to consistently win more battles than they lose while contending with the world, the flesh and the devil. This work is very meaningful to me personally because I have been experiencing a greater barrage of "the fiery darts of the wicked one" (Eph. 6:16). I suspect that he knows his time is short and he wants to do as much damage as he can to the cause of the grace of God in Christ, but I take comfort in knowing that "He who is in you (me) is greater than he who is in the world" (1 John 4:4).

— Earl D. Radmacher, Th.D.
President Grace Seminary and
Bible Institute of the Northwest
President and Distinguished Professor of
Systematic Theology Emeritus, Western Seminary

Over the years my friend Karl Payne has helped me understand spiritual warfare in a way that is both rigorously Biblical and practical. I am excited to see his wisdom now in print for others to benefit as I have.

—Mark Driscoll
Founding Pastor of Mars Hill Church,
Seattle President of the Acts 29 Church Planting Network
President of The Resurgence Missional Theology Network

My friend Karl Payne has written a thoughtful book based on years of study of the Scriptures and personal experience counseling Christians under demonic influence and attack. You need not agree with all the author's positions, but if you trust God's Word then you are compelled to believe that there are powerful demonic spirits at work in the world, and that the goal of

Satan, prince of demons, is to distract, deceive and devour us. Spiritual warfare is a reality, and the person most likely to lose the battle is the one least aware of it. I recommend Karl's book to help you become more aware of our enemies' strategies and to prepare yourself for spiritual combat.

—Randy Alcorn, author of
Heaven and *Lord Foulgrin's Letters*

Books on spiritual warfare usually make me cringe. On one side, some authors write incendiary works that see a devil behind every bush and every sneeze. Inversely, other theological works often ignore the demonic realm completely, as if Satan is simply a metaphor, and not real. This work by Karl Payne is a Godsend. Finally we have a balanced and theologically sound examination of demonic oppression and possession. Karl Payne has written a book that offers hope to the believer, and help for those who struggle with the very real issues of spiritual combat. This book is an indispensible aid to counselors, teachers, theologians and laymen. Buy one for yourself, and another for your church library!

Dr. Ergun M. Caner
President and Dean
Liberty Baptist Theological Seminary and Graduate School

Spiritual Warfare:

Christians, Demonization and Deliverance

Karl I. Payne

CTP

Cross Training Press
Sammamish, Washington

Cross Training Press
21825 NE 9th Street
Sammamish, Washington
98074

ISBN: 9780981752808

Library of Congress Control Number: 2008904484

Scripture quotations taken from the New American Standard
Bible®
Copyright © 1960, 1962, 1963, 1968, 1971, 1972, 1973,
1975, 1977, 1995 by The Lockman Foundation
Used by permission. (http://www.Lockman.org)

Printed in the United States of America by Lightning Source, Inc.

DEDICATION

I want to dedicate this book with love, gratitude and appreciation to:

My Lord and Savior Jesus Christ, who I pray is glorified through its pages and the lives of those touched through it directly and indirectly. To God be the glory, great things He has done.

My wife Gail, who is the greatest gift I have ever received from God on Earth and who has lovingly and faithfully stood beside me through more than thirty years of marriage and ministry. I love you, I cherish you, and I thank you. I still think I got someone else's blessing!

My son Jonathan, who has courageous faith and has known the Savior since he was very young. Walk with God for it is the only thing that will ultimately matter. This world and its tinsel are going to burn to ashes at the bema seat of Christ.

My mom Vida, who has always viewed me through the rose colored glasses that only a mom can wear for her children. Momma, I love you and thank God for you every day.

My dad Holland, who consistently modeled faithfulness, responsibility, persistence, honesty, honor and courage to always stand upon your convictions even if you must stand alone. Poppa, you lost your battle with cancer, but you won the war through Jesus. I still miss you.

My pastor Dr. Lee Toms, who is now with Jesus, and my first spiritual mentor Professor Joe Simmons, who both tirelessly and patiently answered my numerous questions about the Bible and Christian living.

Pastor George Birch and his wife Grace, who introduced me to the "how to's" of successfully and systematically identifying and responding to demonic warfare. Thank you for being willing to sacrificially give away the things you learned on the mission field and in the pastorate at home when so many of your colleagues and friends were afraid to do so. The Christian world owes you both a great debt of gratitude for your courage and faithful service.

My friend Renee, through whose suffering God opened the eyes of a young pastor to the reality of demonic warfare and to the necessity of being able to respond Biblically to it. Through your pain hundreds and hundreds of our fellow brothers and sisters in Christ have been set free from demonic bondage. Your suffering has not been in vain. I still wish I had understood more about spiritual warfare before I met you and your family rather than after.

TABLE OF CONTENTS

FOREWORD

I was very pleased that Dr. Karl Payne asked me to review and endorse his well written book on spiritual warfare. As one who has been involved in Biblical and theological studies and has experienced more than forty years in teaching and counseling in angelology and spiritual warfare, I recognized Dr. Payne's solid Biblical and theological approach as well as the validity of his experience. He presents a valid challenge to all believers in Christ and especially to those concerned with Biblical discipleship to face the reality of demonic oppression and control in the lives of genuine believers. He gives due credit to the reality of physical and psychological factors that affect us, but he challenges laymen and professionals to a Biblical world view that incorporates spiritual factors, especially demonic influence that affects our mental and physical well being.

For those who have been confused and trapped in seemingly hopeless battle with intrusive thoughts and suspicions of insanity, this book offers a very plausible and possible solution. Satan and demons are mind control experts. They insert propaganda and seek to destroy or disable even genuine believers. Dr. Payne offers hope for many seemingly hopeless cases through understanding the enemy's tactics and suggesting a Biblically based defense and counterattack.

With emphasis on the believer's secure acceptance in the grace of God and the righteousness of Christ, the author gives the believer proper perspective on winning the battle for the mind and life. He emphasizes the position and power of the crucified, risen and exalted Lord Jesus as totally sufficient to handle Satan and his host. He instructs the believer regarding his position as being raised with Christ and exalted far above all levels of demonic authority. He suggests the practical steps of recognition of the demonic tactics, confession and renunciation of sin, claiming back the territory surrendered to Satan, and commanding the removal of wicked spirits in the name of Christ.

Payne takes to task those who refuse to consider the possibility of spiritual warfare as ignoring the Biblical evidence and failing to help those in bondage. He cites ignorance of Biblical and clinical evidence as a major cause of this failure. He weighs hard against fear of wicked spirits and fear of men's opinions as deterrents for doing the will of God. Payne says we should not be concerned for our reputation, but for doing the will of God in facing the enemy and freeing the captives. It is not special power or gifts of the individual but the position we have in Christ and the delegated authority from Christ that provide the basis for victory in spiritual warfare.

He claims that those who blatantly state that Christians cannot come under the influence and power of Satan and demons are speaking dogmatically without support of either Biblical or experiential evidence. He does not build doctrine on experience, but he chastises those who claim that Christians cannot be bothered on the basis of faulty exegesis of the Bible or on their lack of recognizing demonization.

He holds that demons actually cannot possess anyone, believer or non believer, in the sense of owning them. Rather demonization refers to an internal type of control to a greater or lesser degree and various manifestations. Christ dealt with demonized persons during His earthly ministry not only to relieve misery but to prove He was the promised Messiah, the Son of God and Savior. He delegated authority to His apostles and to the seventy He sent to heal and cast out demons. His Great Commission delegates authority to all His followers from His ascension to His Second Coming. We are to exercise that authority today in making disciples until He comes again.

Payne's analogies and illustrations are quite clarifying, and his cases studies throw a great deal of light on the reality of spiritual warfare and the benefits of challenging wicked spirits who prey upon God's people. He challenges charismatics and non charismatics to a solid Biblical study and non flashy treatment of demonization. The relief Christ offers is available to us today not due to gifts or personal powers, but through the delegated authority granted to every believer in union with Christ.

The reader should consider the qualifications of the author. This man is a seasoned pastor with an earned doctorate. He has served as a chaplain for an NFL team and has worked with demonized persons for over twenty-five years. He has faced opposition for his stand, even from good Bible believing pastors and professors; but he feels he must speak the truth as God has clarified it to him in Scripture and in counseling experience. He wants us to have workable, transferable principles that have been tested so that we may experience and have others experience freedom in Christ. So he presents in balanced fashion our battle against our three enemies: the world, the flesh and the devil. He would have us aggressively approach this matter of spiritual warfare.

We must take seriously the matters treated by Payne. I believe that pastors, counselors and laymen will benefit greatly from the instruction and challenge in this well written book.

Fred Dickason

PREFACE

The world, the flesh and the devil represent confrontation in three areas: sociological, physiological and supernatural. The Bible discusses all three of these opponents, and all three are real. Yet too many Christians lose more battles than they win and endure their walk with God rather than enjoy it. If everyone could approach spiritual warfare Biblically—like buying a pair of tube socks, one size fits all—then this book would probably not be necessary. But as you already know or will soon discover, a wish, a hope and a prayer are not the best response to attacks from the world, the flesh and the devil. Christians must be strategic in their responses to these three enemies, learning how to fight Biblically and effectively rather than just sincerely.

The book you have in your hands will thrill and encourage some and anger or dismay others. It will no doubt go too far for some and not nearly far enough for others. In one sense, I can't win on this one, knowing this material is going to offend someone. On the other hand, I can't lose in writing this because I do so out of a deep sense of obedience to God and an obligation to share what He's taught me about spiritual warfare over the last twenty-five years. Fear of criticism or rejection keeps many good books from being published and ideas from being shared. The truth is, I no longer care whether my colleagues agree or disagree with my conclusions on this subject. I've witnessed the joy of Christian brothers and sisters being set free from demonic bondage hundreds and hundreds of times. Typically the most grateful people are those who know firsthand what it means to be freed from the mental paralysis, emotional hopelessness and sometimes even physical pain associated with the torment of demonic bondage. And typically, those most upset seem to consistently reject the experience of deliverance as merely superficial or imaginary, while confidently asserting dogmatic opinions about spiritual warfare. Ironically, these opinions are usually based squarely upon their own speculations regarding a subject with which they have little or no firsthand knowledge or experience. This strikes me as curiously superficial, too!

The real truth is that this is one subject that divides sincere Christian men and women across denominations. They might be equally committed to love God and their neighbors as themselves, have received similar Biblical education, study the Bible, be able to work in the original languages of both the Old and New Testaments, and yet still disagree on various points of spiritual warfare. There wouldn't be ambiguity among equally sincere and educated Christians if such a background could clearly resolve all the questions the topic raises in general and about demonic bondage specifically.

But ambiguities do exist, and those ignoring this fact risk appearing to believe that their own opinions should somehow receive more credibility than those of equally sincere and credentialed colleagues who don't share their views. Such theological elitist thinking smacks of pride and is annoying and contemptuous. Ultimately, regardless of where we stand on the subject of spiritual warfare, we need to agree with Romans 14 that we will all one day give an account to the Lord God Almighty, not to each other. Paul's admonition isn't meant as an excuse to quit reasoning together as we agree or agree to disagree. It should remind us that we are all finite servants of God who know only in part and will one day account to the Lord Jesus Christ for everything we say, think and do (Matthew 12:36–37, 1 Corinthians 4:4–5 and 2 Corinthians 5:10–11).

Why write this book now, when I've declined several opportunities to do so in the past? The short answer is that the need is great, and it's past time for Christians to gain a growing understanding of the simplicities, subtleties and complexities of spiritual warfare. I believe I've been given a message that needs to be heard, understood and applied by Christians caught in the middle of spiritual attacks they don't comprehend—and by believers willing to reach out to those desperately in need of encouragement and help.

I was recently forced to face my own mortality while meeting with several medical specialists who were running tests to see if I would be facing a battle with intestinal or stomach cancer. I'm grateful the tests and biopsies showed I don't have cancer. But the weeks of appointments and tests were a timely opportunity to evaluate more than thirty years of ministry. During that period, I was also able to ask and answer a vital question: What messages or lessons would I share more if I found out my race with life was going to finish sooner than later? Two ideas kept occurring to me.

First, besides guiding, guarding and loving my family, the most important assignment God has given me is to continue focusing on transferable discipleship training. So I've renewed my commitment to two areas: (1) To write, teach and preach transferable discipleship lessons, and (2) to continue training disciple makers who will repeat the same process with others by design. My foundation website, (TCTF), at www.karlpayne.org provides transferable discipleship materials and information on this ministry.

Second, God gave me a deep sense of both urgency and peace that it's now time to formally and publicly release the materials on spiritual warfare. I'd already written much of this book but purposely chose to file it for nearly a decade. Like other Christians, I'm responsible for investing my time and talent while I can. The reality is that we're all in the process of dying physically, one day and one heartbeat at a time. Once in a while though, some of us face this reality check in an up front, in your face, urgent manner. I've responded by reaffirming my responsibility to model and promote transferable discipleship. I'm also committed to confronting the subject of spiritual warfare, regardless of what it may cost me by way of personal reputation or criticism.

For many years I disagreed with the position I now believe true. This is primarily because of my own self-imposed ignorance and partly because it was possible to faithfully serve God in ministry for many years without having to consider the subject of demonic warfare personally. A dear friend lying on my living room floor, contorted, eyes crossed, drooling saliva and screaming that her name was something other than her real name changed the luxury of ignoring this subject in a brief, gut-wrenching moment of time. I now believe that such ignorance represents little more than fearful irresponsibility and pride. The time and opportunity to passively sit on the sidelines, content to speculate about this uncomfortable subject is—like the Dodo bird and T Rex—gone.

You certainly may disagree with my conclusions. I pray, however, if you do, that your disagreement be civil and based upon your commitment to Scripture rather than to theological or ideological positions championed regardless of Scripture. My challenge regarding transferable discipleship training is that we know what we believe, that we know why we believe what we believe and that we know how to clearly share what we believe with others. The subject of spiritual warfare is one more area where Christians are responsible to confidently accomplish this.

I personally believe that demonic deception is increasing, even within the Christian church, and that the worst of this deception is still to come. If God allows demonic activity to increase until His return, I believe He will also train up and equip a growing number of His children to faithfully and effectively contend with the powers of darkness who oppose His plans and people. Too many North American churches are well on their way to becoming the same spiritually dead museums as Western European churches.

It's time for Christian soldiers to stand up and contend for the faith once delivered to the saints while we still are able, whether our opposition is natural or supernatural. The alternative is to continue sitting silently in comfort, hoping to blend into a society that's decaying at an increasing rate. We're commanded to live in this world as Christ's ambassadors, shining as lights in the midst of a crooked and perverted world. You can appear politically correct at the expense of being Biblically correct any way you please, but it still represents the compromised sin of disobedience.

God bless you as you stand up to the challenge of learning how to Biblically contend with the world, the flesh and the devil. We are called by God to walk worthy of our calling in Christ and to live as spiritual victors rather than as spiritual victims. Pragmatically speaking, it's time for this positional truth to become a daily reality rather than just an occasional prayer we offer or a song we sing.

ACKNOWLEDGEMENTS

I would like to thank my artist, Mark Dobratz, for all of the creative, thought provoking artwork you have done for me over several decades as a service to God. I have watched you preach sermons through paint that are more powerful and effective than many preachers do through the pulpit. You are a creative genius who loves God and his family and I love, admire and respect you, my brother. Laura, I would like to also publically thank you for sacrificially allowing your husband to have the time away from you and your family to help me with numerous art projects. Effective ministry is usually a team effort, and you two are no different. Again, thank you both!

I would like to thank my editor, Linda Nathan, who has patiently and professionally worked with me to make this book more readable. Your grammatical understanding, insight into the world of demonic warfare, wordsmithing, respectful comments and encouragement have been invaluable to me with this project. I can and will wholeheartedly recommend you and Logos Word Designs, Inc. (www.logosword.com) to anyone looking for a great editor who walks with God. You could not have made this any easier for me, and I thank you.

I would like to thank my literary agent, Les Stobbe, for encouraging me to get this book published one way or another. You are a consummate professional, a godly gentleman, a sincere encourager and a much appreciated friend. Thank you!

I would like to thank Fred Dickason, Stephen Newby, Mark Bubeck, Earl Radmacher, Mark Driscoll, Randy Alcorn, Ergun Caner and the many other wonderful people who have agreed to put their names and reputations on the line by encouraging me to get this material published or by being willing to publically endorse it. Thank you for your support and confidence.

I would like to give a special thanks to Dr. Mark Bubeck, Dr. C. Fred Dickason and your wives for courageously standing on God's word and for sharing the things you have learned about demonic warfare through your books and testimonies. God alone knows how many people have been helped through your obedience to Him, but I am sure the number is legion. Thank you!

Lastly, I want to thank Gayle Cantrell of Lightning Source Inc. who has made the printing of this book a joyful adventure rather than a fretful nightmare. Thank you for the gracious way you have guided me through this process from start to finish.

1

Scripture is Inerrant;

Man-made Paradigms are Not

What would you say to a pastor walking into your office complaining about constantly battling feelings of inferiority, thoughts of suicide and habitually hearing accusatory, debilitating voices telling him he's a loser who will never live up to his potential as a husband, dad, son, child of God or pastor? He tells you he's prayed, fasted, memorized Scripture and studied his Bible, but the ideas, thoughts and voices never release their paralyzing grip on his mind, at least for very long.

Do you tell him he has a chemical imbalance? Do you assume he's obviously schizophrenic because he says he hears voices, and schizophrenics often complain about hearing voices? Do you tell him he's going through a mental meltdown? Do you tell him he's under demonic attack? Do you tell him he's not really a Christian, ignoring the fact he's faithfully and effectively ministered in a large, evangelical church for nearly fifteen years, simply because his experience doesn't fit your theology? Can you help him discern whether his battle is physiological, sociological or supernatural in nature? If your answer to this last question is "yes," you represent a distinct minority, even among Christian leaders, currently living in North America or Western Europe. If you've learned to recognize and distinguish these three types of spiritual warfare, are you also willing and able to show him how to take steps to successfully confront and overcome his particular battles?

What would you tell a minister's wife who tearfully informs you she has a sexual addiction? What do you say when she informs you that she's leaving her family after twenty-seven years of local church ministry with her husband because of her guilt and shame—unless you can help free her of the bizarre thoughts and unrelenting, condemning voices tormenting her daily? Is her problem physiological, sociological or supernatural? How do you know? Medical doctors are available for referral if her problems are physiological, and psychologists and psychiatrists can help when issues are psychological. But what do you do when you learn that years of "professional counseling" haven't accomplished anything except deplete her bank account? She's now convinced that since prayer, fasting, Scripture memorization, doctors, secular counselors, Christian counselors and pastors haven't helped her, there's truly no hope or help from either man or God. Is she doomed to a life of misery like the voices tell her? Would she really be better off dead? The voices tell her that, too.

What do you share with a dad who states that he's afraid his teenage daughter might be involved with demons? He explains that her problems with blasphemous thoughts about Jesus and voices instructing her to kill herself began five years earlier. She has been under a doctor's care and in the offices of both professional Christian and non-Christian counselors for several years, but her mental torment has only increased through the process. The medications she takes only dull the voices, not eliminate them. The mental message she consistently hears is mocking, telling her that she's beyond God's help because nothing can or has eased her pain. She's told that if God really loved her, she wouldn't be going through this suffering and that she's a fool to believe He cares about her. Do you refer her to a private or state operated mental lock-up facility for evaluation and help? She's already been there and left the doctors puzzled, her parents in financial bondage and herself more depressed than when she was first admitted.

What do you tell a strikingly beautiful woman sitting across from your desk who's convinced she's an unlovable, ugly duckling? She's just been flown in from out of state, following a two week hospital stay for attempted suicide. She sheepishly tells you that her ongoing problem is the degrading voices and depressing thoughts she lives with on what seems like an hour by hour basis. These voices or thoughts habitually tell her she's ugly, dirty, too fat, damaged goods, a fool for trusting God because He doesn't really love her, too lazy to read her Bible and too stupid to get anything worthwhile from it when she does try. She further informs you that although she's able to read novels by the hour, when she opens her Bible she can't keep her eyes open more than a few minutes. She now believes that her only hope for true freedom from her mental prison and suffering is by shedding her own blood and ending her life.

The added irony to this story is that this woman is about thirty years old, a tall, riveting, beautiful, professional model that turns heads everywhere she goes. She feels mentally paralyzed, emotionally drained, physically dead or dying, questions her salvation and sanity and is convinced she is unlovable, beyond hope and help and too ugly and weak ever to attract a man of God.

What do you say to a college athlete who's just attempted suicide because of the recurring guilt, confusion and regret she feels over her premarital sexual conduct? She's spent the last three years in a lesbian relationship she now wants to break off because she believes in her heart it's morally wrong. But she fearfully and secretly wonders if she's destined to continue in this lifestyle she now rejects, leaving death her only viable option. Peers and counselors—many of whom assume they're helping or comforting her—tell her that her sexual predisposition is probably genetic, and there's nothing she can do about it except learn to embrace it. These same peddlers of clichés, junk science and moral relativism also assure her that she can best handle her guilt feelings by abandoning her bigoted and antiquated Christian faith, which only makes her feel guilty about something she ultimately can't control.

The mental barrage she faced daily was very predictable. I asked this young lady what I would hear if I could step into her mind and listen, unfiltered. She was embarrassed but also desperate for real help. She told me she constantly heard thoughts and voices in her mind telling her she was a terrible Christian and God really didn't love her. She said she was ugly and that a man would never want her for a wife. She felt dirty inside and mentally tired of fighting a battle she couldn't seem to win, regardless of how sincerely she prayed to God for help or how much she tried to read her Bible.

I've found sexual abuse a very consistent common denominator when counseling men or women who feel compelled to live a lifestyle of premarital or extramarital sexual promiscuity and who also profess a Christian faith. They usually want out of this lifestyle but feel hopelessly trapped within it.

Approximately one year later I ran into this beautiful young woman at a church service. She hugged me and then proceeded to tell me that she was out of her mentally, emotionally and physically guilt-ridden relationship, at peace with God, hopeful and content for the first time in a very long time and growing in her loving relationship with Jesus Christ.

Do you tell the pastor, the pastor's wife, the teenage girl, the professional model and the college athlete that they're all imagining the thoughts and voices that have paralyzed their thinking? We're trained to assume they're either suffering from a mental dysfunction, a physiological imbalance or an over-stimulated imagination. But what if the voices they insist they've been hearing are real?

Is it possible that sincere and well-meaning doctors and counselors, who reject the reality of the supernatural a priori, are actually condemning at least some of their patients to ongoing mental and emotional torment because of their own anti-supernatural bias? Do you tell people suffering through this type of torment that they're just not diligent enough in their prayer time and Bible study? That if they were really serious about walking with God they wouldn't be troubled like this? Do you mentally write all five of these individuals off as weak-willed people who must be unwilling to consistently obey God? Do you tell them their commitment to Christ is also imaginary because you can't reconcile their struggles with your theological suppositions and training?

The individuals I've mentioned are not hypothetical, they are real. All five are professing Christians, as sincere in their commitment to Christ as anyone reading this book. Their stories, unfortunately, are not unique. The situation of the pastor and the pastor's wife may seem a bit more dramatic or unusual because both of these individuals are Christian leaders who have led Bible studies and ministered to others for many years. But the struggles they battled on a daily basis in their minds are a sad reality for many of the parishioners in their churches, who continue to suffer in silence. Why? With few exceptions, Christian leaders are neither willing nor able to identify and confront supernatural spiritual warfare. The mental harassment and demeaning, accusatory thoughts are also the daily reality of many of their former parishioners. These are the growing ranks of members who no longer attend church or attempt to read their Bibles because they're convinced that either they've lost their salvation or Jesus apparently never really came into their lives in the first place. From their tormented perspective, they are fearful, angry, lonely, lost, losers, spiritual shipwrecks, damaged goods, stupid, faithless, fat, ugly, unlovable, unable to love, too stupid to understand their Bibles, and—as they have heard so often—it will never change because God no longer loves them, if He ever did in the first place.

If demonic deception increases as we approach the return of the Lord Jesus Christ for His bride, and I believe it will, then it's past time Christian leaders make an honest attempt to learn how to confront spiritual problems rooted in demonic warfare rather than in mental or physiological maladies. It's easier to avoid supernatural struggles than to confront them because of the fear of being associated with doctrines outside of our comfort zones. It's also more convenient for Christian leaders to refer such troubled individuals to medically trained experts than to admit that we need to be able to provide spiritual answers for spiritual problems that go beyond telling people to pray harder and to read their Bibles more diligently. Jesus and the Apostles clearly taught the reality of supernatural demonic warfare, so why should we be afraid or apologetic about approaching this subject forthrightly?

For more than a decade, I've been asked to collect and systematize my thinking and experiences regarding Christians, demonization and deliverance. Yet until recently I've consistently declined the challenge to publish materials on this particular subject. Why now? First, I believe God has directed me to do so; it's time. Second, these materials are Biblically based, transferable, field-tested, and they work. Third, either the number of demonized Christians is increasing or the reality of this problem is becoming more readily recognized inside the church. Fourth, I don't fit the typical narrow stereotype often associated with deliverance ministry by those who actively oppose the idea of Christians being demonized. I don't drink poison, handle snakes, roll on the floor or throw or break chairs when I speak. God doesn't speak to me through dreams and visions, and I value factual information more than personal feelings. God's Word, the Bible, ends a discussion for me, regardless of how sincerely and passionately the person sharing a different opinion presents his case.

I'm a seminary graduate, an ordained Conservative Baptist minister, an NFL Chaplain, and I've taught classes for high school students, undergraduate college students and seminary graduate students on numerous occasions. My bachelor's, master's and doctor's degrees are all earned rather than honorary, obtained through accredited classroom study rather than the United States Mail Service. I've had several books published that vary in subject content from Christian discipleship to ballistic missile defense and still focus the majority of my ministry time on transferable discipleship and leadership development. I've continued to serve in large, Bible-centered, local churches since 1980 and have never hung a shingle saying, *Exorcist Inside, Full Payment Expected BEFORE God Can Be Contacted, or If You Have the Faith, I Have the Gift.*

I don't know that I can improve on what has already been written on this subject. Devout Christian leaders like Merrill Unger, Mark Bubeck, C. Fred Dickason, Ed Murphy, Neil T. Anderson and Charles Swindoll have all made valuable contributions to our understanding of this topic. However, I believe there is a desperate need to equip more Christians to comfortably and effectively confront the issue of spiritual warfare and to be willing and able to assist demonized individuals. Walking daily with Jesus Christ is a challenge in the best of circumstances. But regardless of the spiritual, mental and physical conflicts challenging our faith, joy and freedom should still characterize a Christian's inner life more than fear, depression, mental torment and the debilitating belief that the human body is a jail not a temple.

Consequently, I think there's still room for at least one more voice in the choir of men and women trying to faithfully and Biblically awaken and educate the North American Evangelical church to the reality and subtleties of spiritual warfare in the twenty-first century. Materials on the world and the flesh are readily available for the person willing to read. But Biblically based materials from Evangelicals on effectively identifying and confronting the devil and his demonic host are harder to find. Fear of the subject itself and a reluctance to possibly be identified with theological and emotional extremism contribute significantly to the seeming boycott or outright rejection and ridicule of this subject by many Christian writers outside of charismatic circles. After having worked with demonized Christians for nearly twenty-five years, I can say with certainty that demons don't care what church you attend or what spiritual gifts you profess to possess. If you want to serve Christ, you're a candidate for their fiery arrows.

I've worked with Christians from charismatic, non-charismatic, liturgical and non-liturgical churches who have all been demonized. Demons are equal opportunity accusers with no regard for or fear of our denominational ties or theological hobbyhorses. They don't care how proud we may be of our religious heritage or the faith of our fathers.

Spiritual warfare is a topic in Christian circles that can easily appear like a swinging pendulum. On one side of the pendulum swing are the groups who refuse to give any credibility to serious discussions regarding satanic/demonic warfare other than hypothetical lip service concerning the most extreme of possible circumstances. There is a natural, rational, psychological or psychosomatic explanation for nearly all problems, they say. And the ones that don't fit their view aren't worth considering. The subjective experience of Christians who would otherwise be considered trustworthy is suspect at best. A more probable cause for such supernatural hysteria, they believe, would lie in the areas of faulty reasoning, emotional excesses, sincere but naive manipulation, poor Bible study methods or, in some instances, fraudulent and deliberate deception.

On the other side of this pendulum are groups that appear to credit or blame everything on the presence of satanic/demonic activity at the expense of common sense and the need to take responsibility for one's own personal actions. According to these groups, demons somehow have evolved from the position of defeated, evil, finite, created creatures into seemingly omniscient, omnipresent, omnipotent beings that possess and control everything from coffee cups to Spirit-filled Christians.

There is another complication in this battle of extremes. Many of our leading Evangelical Bible colleges and seminaries often innocently ignore, deliberately gloss over or even ridicule, the topic of spiritual warfare in general and satanic/demonic conflict in particular. The bottom line is that many prospective Christian leaders leave school and enter their respective ministries as ill-equipped to personally deal with this conflict as they were the day they began ministerial training.

I've lived over three decades as a Christian, served more than twenty-five years in the local church and experienced countless seminars, retreats and serious interactions with fellow Christians. I've found that my personal experience and exposure to this issue at two leading Evangelical schools was similar to that of most of my colleagues. We simply did not discuss the topic of spiritual warfare inside or outside of the classroom. We did discuss the reality of conflict and temptation from the world, the flesh and the devil. And, since the Bible says all three are real, we tried to decide which theory was most consistent with Scripture and our presuppositions concerning the time and fall of Satan and the creation of his demonic host.

However, what we, or at least I, never learned how to do in my classroom training was to identify these three enemies with any certainty or to distinguish their methods in battle. Ignorance is not bliss. It ultimately guarantees we will fail to learn how to Biblically respond to our enemy's attacks with any consistency and confidence. This puts Christian soldiers at a huge disadvantage in battles we face on a daily basis with the world, the flesh and the devil. Our fight is already difficult enough without purposely giving advantages to our opponents.

This book is an attempt to address the topic of spiritual warfare in a simple and transferable manner. It's also my desire to effectively challenge the ineffective two-fold model of "oppression" or "possession" typically used to explain demonic activity. I'm suggesting a shift to a three-fold model, which adds the category of "demonization."

This model isn't new, and I'm not the first Christian championing the need to provide a more accurate paradigm to explain the spiritual conditions of many Christians. There are several compelling reasons to make such a shift:

- ∞ First, it doesn't violate Scripture. In fact, I believe it does a better job incorporating the totality of Scripture on the subject than the status quo.

- ∞ Second, it provides an explanation for a Christian's spiritual battles that allows for confrontation and resolution rather than just definition.

- ∞ Third, it passes the reality test. Demonized Christians who have been set free and learned how to defend themselves from demonic beating attest to its truth.

I offer this approach in the spirit of stimulating fellow Christian soldiers in love and truth so that we can grow together. If brothers and sisters in Christ are able to increase the effectiveness of their ministries by reading and applying these materials on spiritual warfare, then God be praised. We're a body, we need each other, and we should make a greater impact for Christ together than individually.

2

How Did a Non-Charismatic, Ordained Conservative Baptist Minister Ever Begin Working With Demonized Individuals?

I was seventeen years old and heading into my senior year of high school the evening I became a Christian, June 17, 1970. I was already aware I lived in a world in rebellion against God, but the only thoughts I had about war came from watching movies about World War II or the evening news broadcasts focusing morning, noon and night on Vietnam. With so much attention upon free love, the peace movement and drugs, the topic of spiritual warfare wasn't real hot, even among Christians. People were more interested in avoiding war than promoting it, even if the battles were in the human mind rather than in rice paddies.

I assumed the devil and demons were real because the Bible said so, but I didn't understand their strategies or methods of attack. In 2 Corinthians 2:11, the Apostle Paul indicates that the Corinthian Christians were not unaware or ignorant of the devil's schemes and methods. That may have been true for the first century Corinthian Christians, but I couldn't make the same statement for myself or for other Christians I knew.

My only conscious exposure to the devil, demons or supernatural opposition on a personal level was through an incident that happened when I was about nineteen or twenty. It involved a neighbor who claimed to be a healer. I was aware he had a steady stream of strangers coming to his house at all hours, but I'd never asked why they were there or what they were doing.

One Sunday afternoon I tried to explain the difference between being religious and true Christianity to him. During this conversation he told me three men materialized in his bedroom at his call and told him whom he could or couldn't heal. He said that initially he learned to contact spirit messengers through an Ouija board, but that over the years he'd discovered he no longer needed the board to contact these creatures. He also informed me that his study of the *I Ching*, the *Book of Mormon*, the Bible and a book on astral projection all helped him develop his ability to heal people.

I wasn't certain how to respond to this. But I thought as a Christian I should at least try to do something to help my neighbor. Something was clearly wrong with the picture he'd just painted for me. After praying about it for several days, I finally decided it was time to take some action. Walking across the street to his house, I rang the doorbell, firmly convinced that God was big enough to handle any situation and confident that Romans 8:31 was as true now as when Paul wrote it, "...*If God is for us, who is against us?*"

When Fred answered the door, I rather timidly told him I wanted to read some Scripture and test the spirit I suspected was controlling him. I'm sure he was as amused as I was unsure of exactly what I was up to, but he smiled, invited me in and told me to read to my heart's content. First, though, he assured me that everything he did was in the name of "Jesus." I began reading from 1 John 4:1–6, which says:

> *Beloved, do not believe every spirit, but test the spirits to see whether they are from God, because many false prophets have gone out into the world.*

By this you know the Spirit of God: every spirit that confesses that Jesus Christ has come in the flesh is from God; and every spirit that does not confess Jesus is not from God; this is the spirit of the antichrist, of which you have heard that it is coming, and now it is already in the world.

You are from God, little children, and have overcome them; because greater is He who is in you than he who is in the world. They are from the world; therefore they speak as from the world, and the world listens to them. We are from God; he who knows God listens to us; he who is not from God does not listen to us. By this we know the spirit of truth and the spirit of error.

But before I'd even finished the passage, he snapped back rigidly in his burnt orange recliner, and his eyes rolled up until all I saw was white in his eye sockets. I think my eyes were probably wider than his, but I charged on in sincere confusion. I asked to know the name of whatever was controlling my neighbor, and I'll never forget the answer I received.

Something spoke through Fred that I recognized wasn't Fred. It gave me a name I knew was not my neighbor's first, middle or last name. I asked this thing who it served as its lord and master. And it said "Jesus," which surprised me. "Do you mean the Jesus from Nazareth?" I asked.

"No," it said. "Not that one."

I repeated my question. "Who do you serve as lord?"

I still remember Fred turning his head slightly towards me, smiling. Then the word "Satan" rolled out of his lips in a raspy guttural tone. I'm not ashamed to tell you I was scared to death and had no idea what to say or do next. I began calling out my neighbor's name, and he soon came out of his trance-like state as effortlessly as he'd snapped into it. I told him I was going to go find some help and I'd come back. This was so far beyond my comfort zone and limited ministry experience that I had absolutely no idea where to turn or what to do next.

As God's divine timing had it, the original "Bible Answer Man," the late Walter Martin, was in town speaking at a church close to my house on the subject of the Kingdom of the Cults. I'd planned to attend, so I drove to the church and asked Dr. Martin if he would come over to my neighbor's house with me and confront the demons controlling him. After quizzing me, Dr. Martin respectfully declined my request. Understanding now what I didn't then, I think I would have respectfully responded the same way to this type of invitation if our roles had been reversed. He didn't know me or anything about me, and he was in the middle of a speaking engagement. At that time, however, I was certainly disappointed that he wouldn't help.

I went back to Fred's house, but I had no more success helping him than I had earlier in the day. A few hours after I left his house that evening, my neighbor had an apparent massive heart attack. Two weeks later he was dead. The timing may have been purely coincidental, but the incident left me scared and certain I didn't want to step into this arena again, at least by choice. When the family requested an autopsy to try and determine the cause of his death, I asked his wife if she would let me know the final results. Several weeks later she told me that the medical examiner didn't think Fred died from heart complications, but he wasn't certain exactly what killed him. The whole experience left me puzzled, frightened and asking a lot of questions for which I received blank stares, but very few answers from my Christian friends.

My formal introduction to the subject of spiritual warfare began several years later out of necessity rather than personal choice. I attended two fine schools for my formal Bible training. Both of these Evangelical institutions have solid reputations for teaching consistent Bible study methods, and I'm grateful for the privilege of attending each school. Neither, however, at that time even remotely pretended or attempted to prepare students to recognize, distinguish or contend with the realities of spiritual warfare. To be fair, at that time very few Christian undergraduate or graduate schools attempted to formally address the subject of spiritual warfare in any systematic fashion. The hot topics were spiritual gifts and prophecy. More often than not, they simply ignored the subject of spiritual warfare rather than explore or confront it. Discussions I've had since then with alumni of other Evangelical Bible schools and seminaries have consistently confirmed that my experience was the norm rather than the exception.

Immediately after graduating from seminary I accepted my first full time pastorate. In the midst of my second year there, a counseling episode confronted me that painfully exposed how little I really understood about spiritual warfare. I neither sought nor volunteered for the education I was about to receive, but I now understand it was a necessary part of my ongoing training as a pastor/shepherd. God has entrusted me with the responsibility to help protect Christian brothers and sisters from both spiritual and physical predators.

Early one evening a young woman came over to the house to talk with me and my wife. This wasn't unusual. She had been over numerous times to talk with us. Typically, we ended up discussing the same things: the sufficiency of Jesus, the need to walk obediently regardless of our feelings, the power of prayer and the need to learn how to renew our mind and walk controlled by the Holy Spirit. The depression she was experiencing would usually lift, and she'd leave encouraged and determined to be more disciplined and consistent in her Christian walk.

I had no reason to doubt the genuineness of her salvation. She'd expressed a desire to make certain she was a Christian when she was a team member on a summer mission trip, and I'd personally prayed with her. Her parents had both previously been full time vocational Christian workers with Campus Crusade for Christ and were lay leaders in our church.

This particular encounter began about the same as usual. "Jill" let me know how discouraged she was with herself and that she was contemplating giving up once again. To this day, I still believe she wanted to follow Christ faithfully, but in several areas of her life she felt overwhelmed, demoralized and compelled to sin. She constantly fought accusatory thoughts and feelings of worthlessness and failure. Jill was ashamed and believed she'd failed God so often that He could not possibly still love her, even if He once had. Typically I tried to encourage her from Scripture. Repentance, prayer, Bible study, a renewed mind and a disciplined will—that's all it should take for a serious Christian to walk in victory on a consistent basis, right?

I felt certain Jill was a Christian, but I also believed she was weak-willed and deliberately choosing to compromise her faith in Jesus Christ. The only other alternative I was aware of from my training was that she wasn't really a Christian, but I didn't believe that was true.

After we talked a few minutes, I suddenly flashed back in my mind on the conversation and encounter I'd many years earlier with my neighbor who'd claimed to be a healer. Although I still wasn't certain what I was doing or where it would lead, I told Jill I wanted to read Scripture and test the power she said was controlling her. "Okay," she said.

I opened my Bible to 1 John 4, intending to read the first six verses. I never made it through verse six. She was relaxed when I began reading verse one. By verses two or three, her eyes had crossed and rolled back into her eye sockets. Memories of my neighbor, Fred the healer, immediately raced through my mind, and she began screaming profanities at Jesus Christ and me. I was surprised and scared. She then began yelling, "My name is Gaylord," which I knew wasn't true. I began to read more verses out loud, directed at whatever or whoever had taken control of Jill. She reached out and grabbed my Bible. I immediately tried to pull it back but couldn't. She then began shredding it, throwing the torn pages on my living room floor and screaming, "Gaylord hates this book!" She was laughing and mocking when she stopped tearing my Bible. Jill's fingers then contorted, saliva began drooling out of her mouth, and she curled up in a fetal position in the middle of my living room floor.

I called out Jill's name several times and told her to get up and sit back down in the chair. She did, but it was obvious she was fading in and out of contact with me as she glared with eyes so piercing it was at times frightening. At this point I called for my wife to phone her parents, several pastors from our staff and daughter church and two or three of our elders, one of whom was a retired Bible school teacher and career missionary. While we waited for the men to arrive, I tried to talk with Jill. At times I was talking with her, and other times it was apparent I was speaking to something else. She—or it—would periodically tell me I was a fool and that I didn't know what I was doing, and then it would make extremely vulgar remarks about Jesus Christ.

When the men arrived, we began praying and commanding the demon we believed was controlling Jill to leave her. I assumed that a group of pastors and elders would collectively have more power and authority than I had alone. I was also hoping my missionary friend, who said he had worked with this type of thing in Brazil, would show us what to do. He took the lead momentarily, but he had no more success than the rest of us.

The demon crudely cursed Christ and us, mocking and taunting us as we prayed and gave commands directed against it. The louder we prayed and commanded, the louder it laughed and mocked. When we laid hands on Jill and commanded the spirit to go, it simply said *no*, and told us it would never leave because we couldn't make it go. We seemed to be at a standoff, but we couldn't understand why. As I read the Bible, we were supposed to win these types of battles, but we certainly weren't winning this fight, and we knew it.

We spent hours praying and singing over Jill, commanding this thing to leave her—all with absolutely no apparent success. After many hours, we were tired and Jill was exhausted. She lay down on the floor, contorted and periodically glaring at us. Her dad leaned my direction and said, "That is not my daughter; that is an animal." It was apparent to everyone in the room, including the demon(s), that we didn't know what to do.

The demon(s) seemed to enjoy the whole event. One pastor finally said in exasperation, "Faith is the victory. Let's pray, believe and go home trusting that God will honor our prayers." We agreed and began praying, claiming victory for Jill by faith. Jill became unusually quiet, which we took as an indication that our prayers had been answered and she was finally free. Everyone began to thank God for His mercy as Jill and her dad got ready to leave.

As Jill was following her dad out the front door, she turned around and stared at me. Her eyes looked as though they were on fire. She glared at me and wryly smiled but didn't say a word. Then she quickly turned and walked out with her dad. I leaned over to one of the men and said, "She's still in trouble, that thing didn't go." Apparently I was the only one who had caught her parting gaze because the men continued to praise God after she left. I felt absolutely certain though that something was still wrong.

No one wanted to stick around too long. It had already been a long night. But we were puzzled why the evening seemed so humiliating. We questioned why our prayers and commands appeared so ineffective and powerless against a defeated enemy. We also didn't understand why our missionary friend, who said he had worked with this problem before, had no more success than the rest of us. The night was draining and left us with more questions than answers.

The next afternoon I called Jill and asked her to drop by my office at church. When she arrived, she had a smile on her face and began making small talk. I interrupted her after several minutes and told her I wasn't convinced the issue was resolved. Once again Jill became unusually passive and quiet. I suggested we reread 1 John 4 to make sure she was really free of the demonic control. She agreed to do this again. She told me several days later that it had been an active fight to drive her car to the church that afternoon, but that she was determined to get there and see me.

I opened my Bible to begin reading. But before I could even start, she erupted in mocking laughter. Once again her eyes rolled to the backs of their sockets, and her hands and fingers contorted. Men returned, and we began replaying the same process as the evening before. This time though, two staff members from the Billy Graham organization joined us in the battle. They were in town preparing for an upcoming crusade. After listening to a quick summary of the previous evening, they agreed to stay and help us in the confrontation.

Once again the demon(s) seemed able to resist anything we said. After an hour or so of their mocking, one of the two Graham team members mentioned he had just completed a crusade in Calgary and that a pastor there was very comfortable working with individuals troubled by demonic spirits. I obtained his phone number and called him. He quickly shared a crash course with me on working with demonized people. We were learning on the job with small successes, but we were still making little more headway than before the phone call. We were all frustrated and more than a bit puzzled at the demon's ability to resist our commands.

Ironically, on my desk there was a three-page handout from a retired Baptist missionary living in White Rock, British Columbia, dealing step by step with demonic bondage and deliverance ministry. I don't remember how or when I got the handout. One of the men noticed the paper and asked what it was. After quickly looking it over, a Graham team member said, "Let's start at page one and work systematically through the paper."

We did just that, and for the first time the mocking, laughing and swearing stopped. The responses from the demons moved from condescension and arrogance to matter of fact answers, and at times pleading. We saw God accomplish more, in a quiet orderly manner, in the next several hours than we had the entire previous evening.

It was apparent to all of us that we needed an education on spiritual warfare that none of us had received from our formal training or ministry experiences. Jill's father paid to fly the missionary pastor from British Columbia into town to address our staff and elder board on this subject. In the process of getting to know this quiet man of God and his wife, we discovered they had served in Mainland China, before it closed, with the parents of

Billy Graham's wife, Ruth Bell. Coincidence or not, it seemed very fitting after the tremendous part the men from the Graham association played in helping Jill, that the man who eventually provided the expertise we needed had indirect connections with the wife of Billy Graham.

Over the next several weeks, I had the privilege of sitting in with this godly man as he worked with a number of demonized men and women. He patiently tutored me, sharing information he had spent nearly sixty years learning. After he flew back to his home, he graciously remained a phone call away. His availability saved me countless hours of frustration and ineffectiveness as he shared valuable lessons about demonization that he and his wife had learned both overseas and in North America. He calmly answered my questions, and I had a lot of questions to answer.

I'm not in a position to challenge God's perfect plans and sovereign control over time and circumstances in my life or others. Ephesians 2:10 says He has already prepared good work for His children to do. I also understand that as servants of God, our job is to serve Him faithfully, not to question His motives or methods. It was still difficult to see Jill hurting and yet feel so inadequate to help her. She was more than just another student in ministry or parishioner at the church. She had become a friend to me and my wife, and we loved and respected her.

I have some sorrow and regret when I think of Jill and the way our church handled this whole episode. This type of thing just didn't happen in a non-charismatic church, with pastors theologically trained at Dallas and Western Seminaries. We were a church that boasted of a world mission focus of which it could be honestly said, "The sun never sets on the mission ministry of our church." I'm also certain there were members of our congregation who expressed more concern for the church's reputation than for the health and well being of Jill and her family. Things could, and should, have been handled differently. That old adage about hindsight being perfect can be as true of Christians and church meetings as it is of stockbrokers and business meetings. On a more redeeming note, Jill's courageous suffering became a means of motivation, education and training that has allowed hundreds of other Christians to be helped since then. I've lost touch with Jill over the years, but I've marveled how God allowed the pain of one to become a catalyst for the healing of so many others.

If Jill hadn't been the person God used to open my eyes to the reality of this whole area of ministry, then someone else would have become that person. So ultimately I suppose little would have changed other than the name of that first person and my relationship to her. But watching a friend hurt and feeling inadequately prepared to help her was very difficult.

I have continued to train lay leaders, pastors and Christian counselors who have expressed an interest in learning how to work with Christians caught in the clutches of spiritual warfare. Much of the basic material I now share concerning this ministry can be initially traced back to the conversations and training I received from two faithful missionaries who were willing to give away what they had learned, whether considered conventional wisdom or not.

It is my prayer and desire that this book provide clear, simple, transferable materials on spiritual warfare that anyone willing to do his homework and apply it can confidently utilize. If this material is accurate but so complicated it takes a Bible scholar to use it, then that will severely limit its effectiveness.

In this book on spiritual warfare we are going to examine the realities and characteristics of our daily battles with the world, the flesh and the devil. I refuse to focus on one of these enemies at the expense of the other two. It's clear from Scripture that all three members are real. As such, each demands an examination and an explanation. It's admittedly easier to find materials on the world and the flesh than on the devil and demonic warfare, although that gap is slowly closing in Evangelical circles. It is my desire that this book will provide a fair, balanced and Biblical examination of each member of this triad. Furthermore, this book's purpose is to provide practical, transferable principles that God's people can apply on a daily basis as they learn how to consistently and Biblically contend with the world, the flesh and the devil.

3

The Balancing Act

The world, the flesh and the devil: Think of each member of this triad as representing one third of a pie. It's necessary to understand how each piece works if we hope to examine the entire pie thoroughly. Balance is important in life and something we know we should strive for, but it can be difficult to maintain with a topic as emotionally loaded as spiritual warfare. Honest differences over Biblical interpretation and application, personal bias, a priori presuppositions, theological traditions and personal experiences all contribute to the challenge of remaining objective and balanced. It seems that one person's perception of balance is another person's definition of excess or extremism.

Christians sincerely trying to explain all spiritual warfare in mental or physiological terms do a tremendous disservice to the Bible and to the Body of Christ. It's difficult to admit to students, parishioners or clients that, with rare exceptions, Christian ministers and counselors receive little or no practical instruction, preparation or training in identifying and effectively dealing with demonic attack. Providing medical or psychological labels and producing solutions that actually resolve the problems are not necessarily the same.

According to the Bible, the challenges and battles we face aren't always medical or natural in nature. On the other side of this coin, the Bible is just as clear that all of the struggles we confront in life are certainly not demonic or supernatural in nature either.

Jesus clearly recognized the difference between physical disease and maladies, deformation, epilepsy and spiritual demonic bondage (Matthew 4:23–24). He successfully healed all of the above without apparently deferring to one over the other.

> *Jesus was going throughout all Galilee, teaching in their synagogues and proclaiming the gospel of the kingdom, and healing every kind of disease and every kind of sickness among the people. The news about Him spread throughout all Syria; and they brought to Him all who were ill, those suffering with various diseases and pains, demoniacs, epileptics, paralytics; and He healed them.*

We know it is possible to treat many physical challenges, mental disorders and chemical imbalances without resorting to blaming spiritual warfare and demonic spirits. We should be just as aware that the New Testament reveals there are some physical, mental and emotional problems that actually can have a supernatural cause. These may be specifically supernatural in origin or also have a natural explanation (Luke 8:26–29, 13:10–11).

> *Then they sailed to the country of the Gerasenes, which is opposite Galilee. And when He came out onto the land, He was met by a man from the city who was possessed with demons; and who had not put on any clothing for a long time, and was not living in a house, but in the tombs. Seeing Jesus, he cried out and fell before Him, and said in a loud voice, "What business do we have with each other, Jesus, Son of the Most High God? I beg You, do not torment me." For He had commanded the unclean spirit to come out of the man. For it had seized him many times; and he was bound with chains and shackles and kept under guard, and yet he would break his bonds and be driven by the demon into the desert. (Luke 8:26–29)*

*And He was teaching in one of the synagogues on
the Sabbath. And there was a woman who for
eighteen years had had a sickness caused by a
spirit; and she was bent double, and could not
straighten up at all. (Luke 13:10–11)*

Luke was the New Testament author of the Gospel of Luke
and the book of Acts, as well as the Apostle Paul's traveling
companion. He was not only a devout first century Christian leader
but also a trusted and godly medical doctor. He understood the
differences between natural and supernatural conflict, and he wrote
about the reality of both in his two books.

Those quick to explain recurring problems in
strictly medical, mental or physiological terms, or to find a
demon behind every bush, should remember that some of
our battles may be a blending or a combination of both the
physical and the spiritual. The woman bent over by an evil
spirit for eighteen years in Luke 13:10–17 could be an
example of this combination. Genesis 3:1–6 also provides a
clear example from the Old Testament. Take a minute and
read both passages.

*And He was teaching in one of the synagogues on
the Sabbath. And there was a woman who for
eighteen years had had a sickness caused by a
spirit; and she was bent double, and could not
straighten up at all. When Jesus saw her, He called
her over and said to her, "Woman, you are freed
from your sickness." And He laid His hands on her;
and immediately she was made erect again and
began glorifying God.*

*But the synagogue official, indignant because Jesus
had healed on the Sabbath, began saying to the
crowd in response, "There are six days in which
work should be done; so come during them and get
healed, and not on the Sabbath day." But the Lord
answered him and said, "You hypocrites, does not
each of you on the Sabbath untie his ox or his*

donkey from the stall and lead him away to water him? And this woman, a daughter of Abraham as she is, whom Satan has bound for eighteen long years, should she not have been released from this bond on the Sabbath day?" As He said this, all His opponents were being humiliated; and the entire crowd was rejoicing over all the glorious things being done by Him. (Luke 13:10–17)

Now the serpent was more crafty than any beast of the field which the LORD God had made. And he said to the woman, "Indeed, has God said, 'You shall not eat from any tree of the garden'?"

The woman said to the serpent, "From the fruit of the trees of the garden we may eat; but from the fruit of the tree which is in the middle of the garden, God has said, 'You shall not eat from it or touch it, or you will die.'"

The serpent said to the woman, "You surely will not die! For God knows that in the day you eat from it your eyes will be opened, and you will be like God, knowing good and evil."

When the woman saw that the tree was good for food, and that it was a delight to the eyes, and that the tree was desirable to make one wise, she took from its fruit and ate; and she gave also to her husband with her, and he ate. (Genesis 3:1–6)

The woman's ailment had her constantly bent over—a real physical problem. But the text states that a spirit caused this physical problem, and Jesus drove it away. This cured her physical back problem. Genesis 3 records and explains the fall of Adam and Eve from perfection in the Garden of Eden. Do you remember Eve's temptations of the lust of the flesh, the lust of the eye and the pride of life? All of these are natural in nature. But do you also recall who presented these temptations to sin in the first place? Scripture is clear it was Satan, the devil, in the form of a snake. He challenged Eve to ignore God's instructions. He promised her she could become "as god" if she would willfully disobey her Creator and eat the forbidden fruit. Eve listened to a supernatural, spiritual deceiver and then ate of the natural fruit. Her battle was not just natural or supernatural; it was both working in concert.

What's the point of looking at this third alternative? I'm asking—actually pleading—with Christians who have a bad habit of immediately dismissing natural causes or supernatural causes. Please take the time to consider alternatives that may be outside of your personal comfort zones and training. These alternatives may be truer to God's word than polarizing to extremes or ridiculing positions held by equally devout, sincere and educated brethren.

God created natural laws that help govern our universe just as certainly as He created the angelic hosts and life in the sea and on the land. Although sin and death entered the world through the fall, natural laws were at work before and after this tragic event. Natural laws normally have predictable outcomes. The consistency of natural law provides the basis and the rationale for scientific study. Chaos is difficult to predict or understand without the presence of a consistent control supported by something other than chance.

What do natural laws and predictable outcomes have to do with sin, physical disease, demons and people with polarized views on spiritual warfare? Just this. There are realities in life that are true, whether we choose to recognize them or to understand them. The law of gravity will work whether we profess to be theists or atheists. When a human being challenges the law of gravity by leaping off a tall building, that law normally won't stop working regardless of the person's beliefs. It's possible for God to suspend His natural laws if He chooses to do so, and a miracle occurs when He does. It should be remembered though that such miracles were rare in both the Old and New Testaments. Don't assume they're normative or they no longer will represent a miracle. Drug addictions or childish dares won't change the nature of natural laws. Blaming the world, the flesh or the devil for the predictable results of attempts to violate natural laws is as irresponsible as counselors, teachers, doctors and pastors giving advice clearly outside their training and experience.

On a number of occasions I've referred individuals to clinical counselors or medical doctors when I've sensed that their problems weren't spiritual in nature and fell outside my area of training and experience. On a growing number of occasions, I've also had the privilege of working with individuals whom Christian pastors and counselors have referred to me because they recognized that their struggles appeared to fall outside of their own training.

If our concern is truly the well being of those entrusted to our care, then we must have the integrity, security and courage to send people where they are likely to receive effective help, regardless of how this affects our pride. Sometimes that help will come from a medical doctor. At other times the immediate need may be a good marriage or family counselor. There are also occasions where the best help available is in the office of a local pastor or psychologist. It's true there are counselors and doctors who understand spiritual warfare, just as there are pastors who have professional training as counselors and doctors. But they represent exceptions to the norm. Long term clinical counseling and drug dispensing are outside most pastors' training. Spiritual warfare generally and demonic bondage specifically are typically outside the training and experience of the vast majority of clinical counselors and medical doctors. We must be willing to help each other and to learn from each other if our ultimate goal is to provide effective help.

What do you think of when you hear the words "spiritual warfare"? Reactions vary. Some people become frightened and want to avoid the topic. One colleague at church sincerely informed me, "Karl, if you get involved in spiritual warfare they will get you." The "they" were demons. It's certainly wise not to play games with demonic spirits or to enter the supernatural realm with a cavalier or self-sufficient attitude. But it's an insult to God Almighty for His children to allow themselves to be motivated and controlled by fear. Because of Christ, we are supposed to live as courageous victors, not helpless victims.

The reality of spiritual warfare and the need for God's children to live life as victors rather than as victims is not a new teaching just limited to the New Testament. Elisha's fearful servant learned this important lesson and so did the prophet Daniel. Read 2 Kings 6:15–17 and Daniel 10:10–21.

> *Now when the attendant of the man of God had risen early and gone out, behold, an army with horses and chariots was circling the city. And his servant said to him, "Alas, my master! What shall we do?"*
>
> *So he answered, "Do not fear, for those who are with us are more than those who are with them."*
>
> *Then Elisha prayed and said, "O LORD, I pray, open his eyes that he may see." And the LORD opened the servant's eyes and he saw; and behold, the mountain was full of horses and chariots of fire all around Elisha. (2 Kings 6:15–17)*

> *Then behold, a hand touched me and set me trembling on my hands and knees.*
>
> *He said to me, "O Daniel, man of high esteem, understand the words that I am about to tell you and stand upright, for I have now been sent to you." And when he had spoken this word to me, I stood up trembling.*
>
> *Then he said to me, "Do not be afraid, Daniel, for from the first day that you set your heart on understanding this and on humbling yourself before your God, your words were heard, and I have come in response to your words.*
>
> *"But the prince of the kingdom of Persia was withstanding me for twenty-one days; then behold,*

*Michael, one of the chief princes, came to help me,
for I had been left there with the kings of Persia.*

*"Now I have come to give you an understanding of
what will happen to your people in the latter days,
for the vision pertains to the days yet future."*

*When he had spoken to me according to these
words, I turned my face toward the ground and
became speechless.*

*And behold, one who resembled a human being was
touching my lips; then I opened my mouth and
spoke and said to him who was standing before me,
"O my lord, as a result of the vision anguish has
come upon me, and I have retained no strength.*

*"For how can such a servant of my lord talk with
such as my lord? As for me, there remains just now
no strength in me, nor has any breath been left in
me."*

*Then this one with human appearance touched me
again and strengthened me.*

*He said, "O man of high esteem, do not be afraid.
Peace be with you; take courage and be
courageous!" Now as soon as he spoke to me, I
received strength and said, "May my lord speak, for
you have strengthened me."*

*Then he said, "Do you understand why I came to
you? But I shall now return to fight against the
prince of Persia; so I am going forth, and behold,
the prince of Greece is about to come.*

*"However, I will tell you what is inscribed in the
writing of truth. Yet there is no one who stands
firmly with me against these forces except Michael
your prince." (Daniel 10:10–21)*

When God allowed Elisha's servant to supernaturally see
the situation as Elisha saw it, the servant was able to understand

Elisha's courage in the face of danger and the possibility of imminent death. Those fighting for us are far greater in number and strength than those opposing us in heaven or on earth. In the same way Daniel's response turned from fear (vs. 10) to courageous faith (vs. 19) when he understood not only the realities of supernatural demonic opposition from the Prince of Persia, but his supernatural angelic protection provided by God through Michael, the Prince of Israel. Both Old Testament prophets understood a New Testament reality; if God is for you it does not really matter who is against you.

Romans 8:31 and 37 clearly state that through our union with Christ we are more than conquerors whether our opposition is natural or supernatural.

> *What then shall we say to these things? If God is for us, who is against us? (Romans 8:31)*

> *But in all these things we overwhelmingly conquer through Him who loved us. For I am convinced that neither death, nor life, nor angels, nor principalities, nor things present, nor things to come, nor powers, nor height, nor depth, nor any other created thing, will be able to separate us from the love of God, which is in Christ Jesus our Lord. (Romans 8:37–39)*

If God is for us, it really doesn't matter who is against us. Unfortunately, Christians often assume the roles of victims rather than the victors in spiritual warfare. In his classic book on demonization, *The Adversary*, Dr. Mark Bubeck says that fear is the number one reason demons often successfully defeat Christians. Neil Anderson once told me that the number one offender he encountered in his work with demonized individuals was a conscious refusal to forgive others. In effect, the person controlled by fear is actually saying he's willing to give more credence to the devil's threats to hurt those he hates than to Jesus Christ's promises to protect those He loves. The person controlled by bitterness and unforgiveness has learned to justify accepting from God what he refuses to give to his neighbors. At some point, fear and unforgiveness both represent lies, insult God and should not be controlling characteristics of a growing Christian.

For some the topic of spiritual warfare is a game. Comic books, cartoons, daily sitcoms and video games have popularized and trivialized spiritism and spiritual warfare. It becomes a children's game or superstitious drivel for the intellectually infirm. Paradoxically, the growing popularity of New Age religion and the revival of Neo-paganism have made spirituality and spiritism socially acceptable topics many places, particularly if seen as an alternative to Christianity or Judaism. For others the world, the flesh and the devil represent challenges for intellectual sparring rather than destructive enemies we need to confront to help hurting people.

Does spiritual warfare represent a real problem confronting real people? Or is it the preoccupation of simple people afraid to confront their world rationally and practically? Are demons responsible for everything from migraine headaches to nuclear missiles? Or is demonic control so rare that if it ever does occur, it's only among superstitious animists better left to overseas missionaries?

For many, spiritual warfare represents paradoxical confusion and a swinging pendulum. On the one hand, the Bible is straightforward about this topic so it must be true. Jesus certainly acknowledged the reality of spiritual warfare (Matthew 4:1–12, 17:14–20, Luke 13:11–17). So did Paul, the Apostle to the Gentiles (2 Corinthians 10:3–5, 11:1–4,13–15, Ephesians 6:10–18); James, Jesus' half-brother (James 4:7–10); Peter, the Apostle to the Jews, (1 Peter 5:6–9); Luke, Paul's personal physician and traveling partner (Luke 10:17–20, Acts 19:13–20); Jude, another half-brother of Jesus (Jude 6–8); and John, the Beloved Apostle (Revelation 12:10).

The paradoxical confusion is not usually over the New Testament writer's awareness of spiritual warfare, but rather over the relative silence of the Evangelical church in North America about it despite Scripture's testimony to its reality. Why are so many Evangelical church leaders so hesitant to talk about this topic publicly? Why so hesitant to train people to distinguish between the various tactics and warfare strategies of the world, the flesh, and the devil? The short answer is fear. We fear the unknown, and we fear potential theological associations with groups or individuals who abuse this subject. Failure to prepare for spiritual war can, however, be just as irresponsible as excessive preoccupation with the subject.

Is it true, as some say, that the less a person knows or studies about spiritual warfare the less opposition he will face? If this is true, then ignorance really is bliss. In his insightful booklet entitled "Demonism," Chuck Swindoll asks how many good fighters refuse to study how their opponents fight. The obvious answer is none. Fighters who refuse to study film are soon nicknamed "Canvasback Jack" because that's where they're going to be spending most of their time—flat on their backs. Ignorance of a competitor is not an advantage in athletics, business or spiritual warfare.

Demons are organized in their work and respond to the highest delegated authority commanding them. They are also predictably consistent. Their arrogant responses are often an indictment against the church of God rather than a praise. Unfortunately, they seem to feel quite safe around most Christians. And at times they seem so confident they openly attempt to intimidate with challenges and threats those who oppose them.

This is certainly a far different response than what we read about in the New Testament when demons were in the presence of Jesus, Paul, and other early leaders. They were terrified and trembled before these men. Today, at least in North America and Western Europe, they feel free to mock and ridicule.

What is the difference between then and today? Paul, the Apostles and other Christian leaders understood, accepted and exercised their positional and delegated authority in Christ over Satan and his host (Ephesians 2:6; Luke 10:18–20). It seems today that we are often either unaware of our delegated authority through Christ over demons or we are afraid to exercise this authority, even if we intellectually understand the privilege. When we fail to use the delegated privileges we possess in Christ, demons certainly aren't going to volunteer to cooperate to their own hurt. Although they are often predictable, they certainly aren't stupid.

Since 1982, I have had the privilege of working with hundreds of Christians caught in demonic bondage. These individuals have ranged in ages from children to grandparents, in spiritual maturity from new Christians to vocational ministers and missionaries, and in education from high school dropouts to those with earned graduate degrees.

From my limited involvement working with spiritual warfare, stereotypical caricatures of those caught in demonic bondage often have more to do with fearful or arrogant Christians and the fertile imaginations of Hollywood film writers than reality. The media has popularized the notion that people struggling with demons are freaks. Apparently they are all wild-eyed, schizophrenic individuals who stand on street corners and mumble to themselves or sleep in graveyards, buck naked, possess supernatural strength and enjoy terrorizing people foolish enough to wander into their haunts. By painting this extreme picture of demonized people, most of us feel free to ignore the issue. Or else we assume it affects a handful of tormented souls who mostly live in primitive areas overseas.

My experience suggests something different. I've worked with far more individuals struggling with demonic problems who sleep in their homes rather than in their cars or a graveyard. They may battle daily with irrational fears, habitual feelings of inferiority, isolation and rejection, debilitating mental accusation and self-condemnation, and eating disorders. They may experience a seemingly insurmountable battle trying to read their Bible, to pray or to grow spiritually. They may also have frequent thoughts of harming themselves or suicide, struggle with uncontrolled anger, bitterness, unforgiveness or lust. They may feel hopelessly and helplessly controlled by sex, gambling or drug and alcohol addictions. They may also have deep feelings of abandonment and social isolation, typically triggered by the notions that they are either too unworthy to have any friends or few inferiors are worthy of their time, talent or friendship. Very few of these individuals have played with Oujia boards and Tarot cards, howl at the moon or pray to the devil. A person caught in an unrelenting, downward cycle of mental paralysis, overwhelming feelings of depression, guilt and spiritual failure is more typical of the Christians I've worked with than the media's sensationalized stereotypes.

Most of the time demons would rather systematically deceive people in relative silence than draw attention to themselves. If their presence and opposition become too overt, someone might get suspicious and actually try to get help. Blending in is usually a better tactic that typically goes unnoticed and unchallenged. Things are just the way they are and probably always will be. A demonic spirit desires to destroy those Christ loved enough to die for. They usually focus first on trying to keep people from knowing Jesus Christ as Savior and Lord. If they fail in this assignment, their next job is to do everything possible to keep that born-again Christian self-absorbed and ineffective in ministering to others. If they can't keep a person out of heaven, then making certain that Christian doesn't help anyone else get there becomes plan B.

Think about it for a minute. Quiet work often goes unnoticed. When people are asleep on the job or unaware of the source of their problems, they don't look for help. With enough failure, discouragement, and lost time, even Christians can rationalize giving up on themselves and God. They can believe the lies that it just "doesn't work" for them and things will never change.

I'm just no good. Nothing I do ever seems to work out. What's the use of trying? I'll just fail again; it's just a matter of time. No, God this is your fault. If You really loved me, why would I be going though this? If you can't do a better job taking care of me than this, why should I worship you as a loving God? You obviously don't really love me. Christianity isn't good news; it's a lie.

Dozing Christians in denial are easier to attack than trained warriors who've learned how to contend for their faith. If people

get too loud or obnoxious, they may draw attention to themselves
and others. They may even begin to ask questions and to look for
help. Worse, alert Christians are commanded to support and
befriend people in need. Prayer is a powerful double-edged sword.
You can use it both to defend a friend and to attack an aggressor.
From a demon's perspective, quiet, subtle opposition is often more
effective than loud, aggressive harassment.

Learning how to recognize and deal with the world, the
flesh and the devil has very little to do with IQ, spiritual gifting or
personality types. It has far more to do with understanding and
confidently affirming the work Jesus Christ has already
accomplished on a believer's behalf. It involves recognizing the
authority He has delegated to all those who have put their trust in
Him as their Lord and Savior. Consistent victorious living over the
world, the flesh and the devil is possible in Christ, through Christ,
for Christ and because of Christ.

Our victory and delegated authority over demonic spirits
are like our salvation. Although Christ's sin payment and victory
over death is sufficient to save everyone, it is only efficient for
those who obey His commands to believe and receive the free gift
He purchased for them. In the same way, although Christ has
delegated authority to every Christian over all the powers of the
enemy (Luke 10:18–20), only those Christians who exercise this
authority will realize the awesome victory. Gifts received with joy
but left unopened are of very little value.

> *And He said to them, "I was watching Satan fall*
> *from heaven like lightning. "Behold, I have given*
> *you authority to tread on serpents and scorpions,*
> *and over all the power of the enemy, and nothing*
> *will injure you. Nevertheless do not rejoice in this,*
> *that the spirits are subject to you, but rejoice that*
> *your names are recorded in heaven."*

Demons are like bullies. They feed on fear. As long as you
choose to give your lunch money to the school bully, he'll continue
to demand it. What happens when you finally stand up to him and
say that the only way he'll get it is by fighting for it, that you have

a stick in your hand and your big brother is near? He will usually turn around and take someone else's money. Bullies are cowards who don't really want to fight. They typically use intimidation, hoping a fearful person will give them whatever they want without a struggle.

When you walk onto the schoolyard with your older brother who's much bigger and stronger than the bully, will that bully attempt to take your money then? No. But if he can talk you into leaving your brother's protection, or if he can taunt you with lies or shame you to turn your back on him—"You're a momma's boy, you're a wimp who has to have your brother stick up for you, your brother hates you, you're bothering your brother, he doesn't really want to be stuck with you"—what happens? You're going to miss more lunches.

When the bully leaves you alone, is it because he's afraid of you or of your brother? Your safety isn't dependent upon your own personal strength but upon your brother's fighting ability. Jesus Christ is our big brother. He's always available through His presence and prayer to help us, and He's never lost a fight. Even His crucifixion and resurrection demonstrated His victory over sin and death (Col.2:13). Satan and his demons will taunt and call names; they'll try anything possible to talk us into walking away from the safety of our big brother, Jesus Christ. If we choose to leave Him at home or tell Him we don't need His help, we'll quickly find out who really intimidates the bully and who he's hoping to isolate for a fight.

Several years ago a boy several years older than my son decided he could kick, hit and intimidate my boy before our Wednesday evening Awana program. Jonathan was in second grade at the time. One day he told me he no longer wanted to attend Awana. This surprised me because he'd always enjoyed it. When I asked why he wanted to stay home, he told me about the trouble he was having with "a big boy" named "Billy." Billy the bully was in fourth grade. I made it a point to arrive early at one of the next Awana meetings so I could introduce myself to Billy. I walked into the gym with Jonathan at my side, and he quickly pointed Billy out to me. I asked Billy if he really thought it was okay for him to kick and hit my son. Billy was scared and struggled for words. I told him if I ever received another report that he was hurting my son, I'd get personally involved in the situation. I said I'd begin with a talk with his mother, who was a student in one of my classes. He promised he would never hit or kick my son again, and I made sure he kept that promise.

Billy had absolutely no fear of my son. But he was sure scared of me. He understood that if he started a fight with my son that he was really starting a fight with me and his mom. He was smart enough to realize he couldn't win that fight, even though he was bigger and stronger than my son. Jonathan instinctively understood that as long as he stayed close to me he could count on my defending him. He had nothing to fear from Billy.

Demons are subject to believers through the authority of Jesus Christ. Although they have no fear of believers personally, they are terrified of the One who walks with us. Christ has promised that no one and nothing, natural or supernatural, can ever separate us from His love (Romans 8:35–39).

> *Who will separate us from the love of Christ? Will tribulation, or distress, or persecution, or famine, or nakedness, or peril, or sword?*
>
> *Just as it is written,*
>
> *"FOR YOUR SAKE WE ARE BEING PUT TO DEATH ALL DAY LONG; WE WERE CONSIDERED AS SHEEP TO BE SLAUGHTERED."*
>
> *But in all these things we overwhelmingly conquer through Him who loved us.*
>
> *For I am convinced that neither death, nor life, nor angels, nor principalities, nor things present, nor things to come, nor powers, nor height, nor depth, nor any other created thing, will be able to separate us from the love of God, which is in Christ Jesus our Lord.*

The verse 1 John 4:4 is a reminder of our victory and the rationale behind it. "You are from God, little children, and have overcome them; because greater is He who is in you than he who is in the world." A Christian confronting a demon on his own merit or authority would be even more foolish than my boy attempting to intimidate "Billy" on his own merit or authority. But a Christian confronting a demon in the *name* and *authority* of the Lord Jesus Christ should be as comfortable and confident as my son felt walking into the gym, side by side with his dad. As Christians who understand our delegated authority over the powers of darkness, we win because He has already won. His victory assures our victory over the world, the flesh and the devil, as long as we obediently walk hand in hand with Him.

Why run from a bully or give him lunch money when we know big brother will take care of that bully upon request? Likewise, why should a Christian be controlled by fear of the devil and his demons when our big brother, the Lord Jesus Christ, has already beat their champion, and has promised to stand up for us anytime we ask? Paul understood this when he penned Romans 8:31. "What shall we say to these things? If God is for us, then who is against us?" Paul is saying that it doesn't really matter who is against us as long as God is for us. The message is consistent and clear. We can win because He has already won!

I was walking through a college quad when a Satanist who had heard me speak earlier that day approached and told me I should turn my back on Jesus Christ and follow his master, the "Dark Lord." He challenged me to look around and see which side was winning the spiritual battle on earth. He was serious. (Are you aware that Satanists have evangelists, too?)

I told this young man I had no desire to serve a loser, which surprised and angered him. I reminded him that our respective masters had already battled at Calvary, and my master won that war. I let him know that as far as current world affairs go, things are not always what they appear. The last chapter of the book has been written, and it says that Christ and Christians are the side that wins. I asked him why he would choose to follow a lesser authority that is ultimately lost when it's possible to be loved by the highest authority who has won. He turned his back on me and walked away.

Several months later he called and told me he was bleeding because his master had demanded a blood sacrifice. I thought he was going to bleed to death while we were talking on the phone. Fortunately, I was able to alert authorities who found him still alive. Later I visited him in the psychiatric hospital where he'd been committed. I tried to help him understand that whereas his master had demanded he sacrifice his blood to demonstrate obedience, my Master had willingly shed His own blood because of His great love for me. I had the privilege of going through the gospel with that man before I left, and he committed his life to Jesus Christ.

Christians are on the side of victory through the merit of the Lord Jesus Christ. This is why James and Peter tell us to resist the devil rather than to run from him (James 4:7–10; 1 Peter 5:6–9). Our confidence and victory are not in our own resources or strength. The King of Kings and the Lord of Lords delegates our authority and victory. The Christians' battle with demonic spirits is not ultimately "them against us." The real battle is between our master, Jesus Christ, and their master, Satan. The good news is that our Master already won this war at Calvary (Colossians 2:13–15). Christians who fear a fight with demons don't understand their delegated authority in Christ. They also misunderstand who is ultimately doing the actual fighting.

When I command demons to leave a person, I always do so in the name and the authority of the Lord Jesus Christ. On occasion the demons have protested. They ask, "By what authority are you commanding us to leave?" If I said it was in my own authority or power, they would mock me and anyone else in the room. When I calmly respond that my Savior, the Lord Jesus Christ, delegates my authority, they comply quickly as long as their ground or authority to demonize the individual is gone. The chapters dealing specifically with demons and deliverance clearly explain the concept of "ground."

We need to praise God for Evangelical writers and leaders who have recognized the need, and accepted the responsibility, to equip the saints to confront this subject rather than to run from it— or worse, to define it away. We also need to uphold them, their families and their ministries in prayer. We should do this regardless of denominational differences, as long as they serve the Lord Jesus Christ as Savior and Lord and affirm the Bible's inerrancy. "I am of Paul," and "I am of Peter," and "I am of Apollos," and "I am of Christ," still represents sin, even if it is sincere. As one nationally known Evangelical pastor told me after an evening service, "I believe that as demonic deception increases with the end drawing nearer, it makes sense that God will raise up more Christian leaders who understand spiritual warfare, to help equip His church for the battles." I believe this pastor's assessment is correct.

There's always more to learn and a better mousetrap to make. But you don't have to know everything about the Christian faith to contend for the faith, once delivered to the saints. You shouldn't be deceived into believing your authority to contend in this area depends upon your education or your doctrinal credo. Working with demonized men and women is just one more ministry area a Christian should take seriously and approach forthrightly. It's not more or less important than other areas of ministry where we must help equip Christian warriors.

When I first began working in this area of ministry, it was sometimes lonely. Furthermore, many Christians considered it naive deception, deliberate fraud or chaos and confusion. In some restricted circles controlled by tradition and theory rather than Scripture, and where ministry doesn't have to pass a reality test, this opinion hasn't changed much. I remember James Dobson once saying that we Evangelicals owed an apology to the Roman Catholic Church for allowing them to stand alone for so long against the practice and legalization of abortion. Could a parallel be drawn in relation to the subject of spiritual warfare between charismatic and non-charismatic churches?

As Christians, we're on the same team. That is, unless we're supposed to have a greater loyalty to denominational creeds or personal experiences than to our Savior, the Lord Jesus Christ. Maybe we should think about the question, "Has Christ been divided?" once again. The fact is that our God and His Word are bigger than all manmade theological systems that help systematize our core beliefs. God is never the author of confusion. The notion that we can accomplish more for the cause of Christ complementing each other instead of competing against each other still rings true (1 Corinthians 3:1–8).

> *And I, brethren, could not speak to you as to spiritual men, but as to men of flesh, as to infants in Christ.*
>
> *I gave you milk to drink, not solid food; for you were not yet able to receive it. Indeed, even now you are not yet able, for you are still fleshly. For since there is jealousy and strife among you, are you not fleshly, and are you not walking like mere men?*
>
> *For when one says, "I am of Paul," and another, "I am of Apollos," are you not mere men? What then is Apollos? And what is Paul? Servants through whom you believed, even as the Lord gave opportunity to each one. I planted, Apollos watered, but God was causing the growth. So then neither the one who plants nor the one who waters is anything, but God who causes the growth. Now he who plants and he who waters are one; but each will receive his own reward according to his own labor.*

We need each other and should be stronger in unity than fractured in isolation. To that end, if the things I've learned can help others battle more effectively against the world, the flesh and the devil, then the 2 Timothy 2:2 process will continue to the glory of our great God and Savior, the Lord Jesus Christ.

4

The World:

External Solicitation to Sin

I would like to state at the outset of this study on the world, the flesh and the devil that it is my sincere desire to appeal to thinking minds rather than to curiosity. Thus, I have consciously sought not to sensationalize and dramatize the topic of demonic warfare in contrast to our struggles with the world or the flesh. The world, the flesh and the devil are each real, and each represents one third of the spiritual warfare pie that Christians must learn to recognize and confront. Demonic or supernatural warfare represents only one third of the battle we face as soldiers of Christ, no more and no less. This third of the pie may seem more dramatic or frightening than the world or the flesh, but in actuality each piece of this pie represents opponents equally capable of destroying our testimony for the Lord Jesus Christ. Consequently, to ignore or to glorify one part of the warfare pie at the expense of the other two is a tragic mistake. I have consciously tried not to make that mistake in addressing this subject.

Christians who desire to walk consistently in victory need equipping to identify and confront all three types of opposition they will face while serving the Lord Jesus as His soldiers and ambassadors. That said, let's examine the first piece of the spiritual warfare pie Scripture identifies as the world.

*You adulteresses, do you not know that friendship
with the world is hostility toward God? Therefore
whoever wishes to be a friend of the world makes
himself an enemy of God. James 4:4*

*Do not love the world, nor the things in the world. If
anyone loves the world, the love of the Father is not
in him. For all that is in the world, the lust of the
flesh and the lust of the eyes and the boastful pride
of life, is not from the Father, but is from the world.
And the world is passing away, and also its lusts;
but the one who does the will of God abides forever.
1 John 2:15–17*

*For God so loved the world, that He gave His only
begotten Son, that whoever believes in Him should
not perish, but have eternal life. John 3:16*

These are familiar verses that many of us have read many
times, and some of us have even memorized them. Several years
ago a child asked me, "Why am I supposed to consider the world
my enemy if God loved it enough to send His Son to die for it?"
This is a fair question for any thinking adult, but I thought it was a
profoundly insightful question for an eight-year-old boy and one
that could indeed appear confusing at first glance. If God loves the
world why should I hate it? "You adulteresses" is pretty strong
language.

The term we translate "world" comes from the Greek word
kosmos. Carl Sagan popularized the term "Cosmos" through his
television program by the same name. We could argue whether his
program was primarily educational or pseudoscientific propaganda
for a worldview known as materialistic naturalism. But we can't
deny that he did an effective job popularizing the term *cosmos*.

In New Testament times the Greek word kosmos had
several distinctly different meanings depending upon the context of
its usage. According to *Vine's Expository Dictionary Of Old and
New Testament Words,* this word denoted:

(1) the Earth, e.g., Matthew 13:35; John 21:25; Acts 17:24; Romans 1:20;

(2) the Earth in contrast to heaven, 1 John 3:17;

(3) by metonymy for the human race, mankind, e.g. Matt.5:14; John 1:9, 3:16;

(4) a term to distinguish Gentiles in contrast to Jews, e.g., Romans 11:12,15;

(5) the current condition of human affairs, in alienation from and opposition to God, e.g. John 7:7, 8:23, 14:30; 1 Corinthians 2:12; Galatians 4:3, 6:14; Colossians 2:8; James 1:27; 1 John 4:5; and

(6) the sum total of our possessions, e.g., Matthew 16:26; 1 Corinthians 7:31.

How do you explain God's Word instructing Christians to consider the world our enemy when God loved the world enough to die for it? The puzzle's solution comes when we understand that the Greek language used the same word "Cosmos" in a variety of ways. When God speaks of loving the world, the word is a synonym for mankind. When He warns Christians not to love the world, He is speaking of an organized system opposing Him.

It is true that God loved the world (mankind) so much that He sent His only begotten Son to die for it. It is also true that if we love this world (a system in rebellion against God), we can't also love God with our whole heart.

God has provided the possibility of salvation for men and women, not for rocks and trees or for a system in active, rebellious opposition against Him. An impersonal system cannot confess Jesus as its personal Savior. But men and women caught in the clutches of that system certainly can.

I understand that I am not to give myself sacrificially to a system in rebellion against God and that if I do it indicates that I do not love God as I ought to. But doesn't the Apostle John's admonition in 1 John 2:15–17 assume that I can identify what this system is and understand how it operates? Where does the Bible clearly explain what this system is and how it works? Look again at 1 John 2:16.

What distinguishable elements make up the world system? *For all that is in the world, the lust of the flesh and the lust of the eyes and the boastful pride of life, is not from the Father, but is from the world.* The world system, which is in opposition to God, consists of the lust of the flesh and the lust of the eyes and the boastful pride of life. But what are they? We can read about some concepts more easily than explain them. And just because I can identify these entities does not mean I know how to personally contend with them.

If someone asked you to explain the concepts of the lust of the flesh, the lust of the eyes and the boastful pride of life to your son, daughter or friend, how would you do it? When you tell someone he must not love the world, you are Biblically correct. But if he doesn't understand what you mean by the term "world," how helpful is this instruction even if it is correct?

The Lust of the Flesh

What is the lust of the flesh? A simple way to explain the lust of the flesh in a context of opposition from the world is as an external proposition designed to trigger a physiological response in our mind and body. Billboards, skin flicks, musical lyrics and media advertisements all represent avenues through which sin can externally solicit us through the lust of the flesh.

What is the first thing that comes to your mind when you read "controlled by physiological urges"? Probably a good first guess would be sex, pornography or some other types of sexual titillation programmed to excite sensual reactions. Is it possible for a person to become enslaved to sexual gratification and turn a good gift God gave His children, in the context He designed it for, into something hurtful? Yes it is. We are living with the destructive results of a casual hedonistic understanding and exercise of human sexuality.

Broken vows and marriages, single parent families, abortion on demand, sexually transmitted diseases, date rape,

AIDS, sexually suggestive advertisements, a multibillion dollar pornography industry that exploits men, women and children, an increasing teenage birth rate, the promotion of premarital or extramarital sexual activity and so forth are all tangible examples of physiological urges controlling men and women.

But battles with pornography, lust and illicit sexual desires are not the only fights we have when contemplating being controlled by physiological urges. How many of us are willingly, and knowingly, shortening our lives by failing to control and discipline our eating habits? Natural, healthy foods are in these days, and fattening foods are out. But the church still overlooks the sin of gluttony. The same person who declares that we should ban smoking in public buildings because it represents a health hazard to our bodies, which belong to God, has no difficulty navigating his already overweight body to the front of the local smorgasbord trough to inhale enough food to adequately feed two or three people. Excuses about big bones and slow metabolism often seem to get more consistent exercise than our bodies.

Alcohol abuse, chain-smoking cancer-producing cigarettes, eating disorders and drug addictions are obvious battles with the lust of the flesh. Alcohol abuse, drug addictions, nicotine-stained fingers and secondhand smoke inhalation are no longer socially acceptable. As such, most people would agree that they represent potential problems we need to address. But how many people have also allowed themselves to become physiologically and compulsively hooked on other habits deemed socially acceptable regardless of their controlling effects? How much starving, bingeing and exercising must young women do before we recognize that they are slowly killing themselves as they compare their bodies with Hollywood's silicon models of perfection? These celluloid men and women are neither perfect nor content. Just ask them. Actors and models chasing their fading illusions of perfection or a competitive edge make plastic surgeons wealthy. Unfortunately, the slick marketing of artificial lies is killing the hopes, dreams and lives of real people. People are buying the lie with a smile and dying in the process. Tragic!

When the lust of the flesh controls me, the Holy Spirit is no longer controlling me. Some of our battles with physiological urges are obvious, and some are more subtle. Galatians 5:19–23 partially lists the fruit or evidences of a life the flesh controls (19–21) and the life the Spirit controls (22–23). The Bible commands us to walk controlled/filled by the Spirit and to refuse control or mastery by anyone or thing except Jesus Christ. *It's only natural* is an excuse for lust-controlled living that those professing God lives in them should not utter or accept.

The Lust of the Eyes

What is the lust of the eyes? And what is the difference between this and the lust of the flesh? The lust of the eyes focuses squarely upon our desire to have beautiful things, which we believe we must have for contentment. By definition, both the lust of the flesh and the lust of the eyes in the world's context deal with external solicitations to sin. A billboard displaying a scantily dressed body attempting to sell anything from breakfast cereal to fast cars might represent the lust of the flesh. The same billboard could represent the lust of the eyes with a winning lotto ticket, a dream house or a rose. The message is clear. You need this. You deserve this. You cannot be content living without this.

Beauty really is in the eye of the beholder. Flowers, paintings, houses, boats, cars, clothes, window shopping, hair, skin tone, jewelry, CDs, books, web surfing online or even Ebay can all potentially represent a person's battle with the lust of the eyes. It is out there, and someone else has it. I don't have it, and I want it. I cannot be happy or content until I get it.

Words like jealousy, covetousness and envy help describe the motivations of the lust of the eyes. People struggling with this lust are typically very aware of what God has provided for others but unaware and unappreciative of what God has done, or is doing, for them. This person's vocabulary may contain the words thankfulness and gratitude, but they are seldom a consistent characteristic of his or her daily lifestyle. You have it. I want it. God is holding out on me. When I get it then I will be happy too.

What is the real difference between a person who makes a lot of money and allows it to control him and a person who hopes to make lots of money and allows this compulsion to control him? Is either individual's focus and passion seeking first the kingdom of God and doing His will? Greed—*I need more*, and envy—*I want what you have*, both fail to promote contentment.

Envy is a terrible sin. This is true whether in a teenager looking at the perfect bodies of professional models or in a pastor praising God for his "quality" ministry as he attacks mega-church pastors and their growing congregations.

The Boastful Pride of Life

What is the boastful pride of life? 1 John 2:16 clearly states that it is a part of a world system in rebellion against God. How do you explain it to someone else? Two words help me remember how to explain the concept of the boastful pride of life: *selfish ambition.*

Luke 12:13–21 illustrates the idea of selfish ambition or ambition out of control.

> *Someone in the crowd said to Him, "Teacher, tell my brother to divide the family inheritance with me."*
>
> *But He said to him, "Man, who appointed Me a judge or arbitrator over you?"*
>
> *Then He said to them, "Beware, and be on your guard against every form of greed; for not even when one has an abundance does his life consist of his possessions."*
>
> *And He told them a parable, saying, "The land of a rich man was very productive.*
>
> *"And he began reasoning to himself, saying, 'What shall I do, since I have no place to store my crops?'*

"Then he said, 'This is what I will do: I will tear down my barns and build larger ones, and there I will store all my grain and my goods.

'And I will say to my soul, "Soul, you have many goods laid up for many years to come; take your ease, eat, drink and be merry." '

"But God said to him, 'You fool! This very night your soul is required of you; and now who will own what you have prepared?'

"So is the man who stores up treasure for himself, and is not rich toward God."

In this parable Jesus tells a story about a very successful farmer. As his field production increased so did the size of his barns. Apparently, at some point he decided he had it made. Maybe he was voted farmer of the year. He felt it was time to kick up his feet, relax, eat, drink and be merry. Jesus told the listening crowd that at this point God called the man's life to account before Him.

Although recognized as a successful man from a human perspective, Jesus' eternal point of view judged him bankrupt. The man had traded eternal life for time, temporal trash for eternal treasure, and all probably with his neighbor's envious approval.

God certainly has a different perspective on success and greatness than many of us do. According to Jesus, the greatest leader is the servant of all, not the individual who lords his position over others with pretense and pomp. (Matthew 20:17–20) Like the rich farmer, we typically view success as an excuse to retire and live for ourselves. Biblically speaking, success is the faithful accomplishment of a stewardship granted from God for service to others. To whom much is given, much is required. Be faithful in small things, and He will entrust you with more. Fail your stewardship in small matters, and even what you have will be taken and given to another. The rich farmer would fit into our culture easily with the thinking and attitudes he displayed. He was culturally and politically correct. But Jesus called him a fool.

Is there anything wrong with a person being ambitious? No. From a Biblical perspective ambition can be the difference between a man having crops to harvest and eat or a person standing on a corner, guitar and sign in hand, begging for food and money. Ambition can help separate the wise man from the fool. In this context, however, the word "selfish" qualifies ambition. Ambition can be healthy. But selfish ambition is self-serving and self-centered. Selfish ambition says, *I have my plans, and I am going to make sure they happen with or without God's blessing or intervention.* Christians controlled by selfish ambition will usually pray about God's will after they have decided a matter and are looking for His confirmation.

> *I'm going to be a successful entrepreneur who owns his own company. I want to work for myself, not someone else. After my business succeeds I'll tithe a portion of my earnings to the work of God. When things slow down a little bit I hope to get back to church and find a time to study my Bible. God understands. He knows that if I don't make it big financially now I won't be able to give as much for His work later.*

> *I'm going to get married. I know the Bible says I'm supposed to marry a Christian, but this person is nicer than any Christian I've ever dated before. I'm sure I can convince him to go to church with me. I just know he'll become a Christian real soon. Besides if I break up our relationship he may never meet another real Christian woman. He might think I consider myself better than him and that would leave a bad testimony. It could turn him off to Christianity forever. I believe it's my job to be a missionary in this relationship. God understands. We will be a powerful couple for His work in the future.*

> *God told me to divorce my wife. She's holding me back from being the Christian He wants me to be. I'd be better*

*off without her, and she would probably be happier, too. I
need a wife who will support me, not hinder the work God
has called me to accomplish. The kids would be better off
this way, too. They'll still be able to see me at holidays and
during the summer. I'm sure they'll be happier not seeing
us argue all the time. I know God wants me to be happy,
and He's a God who forgives.*

There's nothing wrong with making money and excelling at
your job. Likewise, God instituted marriage so He must believe it
is honorable. The real issue here concerns timing and obedience.
Do we consult God for His opinion before or after we make
decisions? Do ends justify the means? Are we to sin that grace may
abound? Romans 6:1–2 says "no." But sin is so easy to rationalize.

In confronting situational ethics we do not believe a
righteous end justifies an unrighteous means. We could argue that
an unrighteous means cannot produce a completely righteous end.
In confronting major decisions like our vocations or whether or not
to marry or divorce, how often do we allow the applause of people
to drown out the voice of the Holy Spirit?

Plans that leave God out are foolish and represent selfish
ambition or ambition out of control. We can make plans, but God
is the one who ultimately guides our steps. How many times does
selfish ambition motivate our decision-making process because we
doubt God's goodness and His promise to work all of our
circumstances for good because we love Him and are called
according His purpose?

Have you ever considered how all three of these worldly
attacks confronted Eve at the same time? Do you sometimes
wonder if we are too hard on Eve? She not only didn't have
parents and grandparents to support and encourage her, but
apparently she also had a husband who was far enough away in her
time of temptation that the serpent felt safe propositioning her to
rebel against God. Take a moment and reread Genesis 3:1–7.

*Now the serpent was more crafty than any beast of
the field which the LORD God had made. And he*

said to the woman, "Indeed, has God said, 'You shall not eat from any tree of the garden'?"

And the woman said to the serpent, "From the fruit of the trees of the garden we may eat; but from the fruit of the tree which is in the middle of the garden, God has said, 'You shall not eat from it or touch it, least you die.'"

And the serpent said to the woman, "You surely shall not die! For God knows that in the day you eat from it your eyes will be opened, and you will be like God, knowing good and evil."

When the woman saw that the tree was good for food, and that it was a delight to the eyes, and that the tree was desirable to make one wise, she took from its fruit and ate; and she gave also to her husband with her, and he ate. Then the eyes of both of them were opened, and they knew that they were naked; and they sewed fig leaves together and made themselves loin coverings.

Do you see how Satan, Eve's ultimate source of temptation, utilized all three worldly avenues when he propositioned her to rebel against God? Do you remember how we defined these avenues as 1 John 2:15–17 describes them? We can simply remember that external propositions designed to trigger physiological urges make up the lust of the flesh. The lust of the eyes focuses upon our desire to obtain beautiful things others have and we want. And the boastful pride of life deals with selfish ambition. We make our plans first and consult God about them later.

When the woman saw that the tree was *good for food* (**lust of the flesh**), and that it was *a delight to the eyes* (**lust of the eyes**) and that the tree was desirable *to make one wise* (**boastful pride of life**), she took from its fruit and ate. Satan, the father of lies and the prince of the air, worked directly through all three external worldly gates 1 John 2 describes.

Does this seem complicated? For some people, warfare with the world, the flesh and the devil seems extremely complicated. For others it is profoundly simple. The good news regarding warfare is that if we faithfully study God's Word, as God commands approved workmen to do, we do not have to feel overwhelmed by our opposition. God's word is truth, and truth sets people free.

We are supposed to win more battles than we lose, and the good news is that we can. Victorious Christian living need not be theoretical. It should be the ordinary testimony of all God's children, not the extraordinary witness of a few chosen saints.

The bottom line in Genesis 3 is that Eve got ganged up on. Her attack was not just on one front or by one enemy. Eve's temptations provide a clear picture of a believer's potential battle with the world and Satan simultaneously.

Warfare can be blatant and obvious. But sometimes it can seem subtle and complicated. Have you ever noticed what Satan's first line of attack was when he approached Eve? Some things don't change much, even over a period of several thousand years.

Satan attacked Eve's belief that God is good. He didn't tell her that God hated her. He didn't tell her that she had to work for His acceptance or that she wasn't religious enough to please Him. The Evil One intimated that God was failing to watch out for her best interests. It's as though he were whispering in her ear:

> *God isn't really concerned about your best interests. He doesn't want you to eat from the fruit of this tree because He knows if you do you'll become just like Him and no longer need Him. God's trying to hold you back from being all you can be because He wants to control you. He's evil and selfish, not good and benevolent. Go on, don't be stupid. Go ahead. You're naive to believe He's watching out for you. Don't let Him get away with this. Use your head. Stand up for yourself.*

Does Satan use this same tactic with Christians today? Yes he does. Sometimes the attacks are more subtle, but often they are blatantly obvious. Our inability to recognize this type of attack is an unfortunate indication of just how far we have slipped in understanding Satan's methodologies and strategies.

How can you believe God loves you when things that are unfair and unjust happen to you? If God really loved you and watched out for you He would intervene. Don't you understand? You're so naive.

You're never going to find a spouse. God has forgotten you. If you don't take things into your own hands you're going to end up single and lonely. Go ahead, go for it. If God really cares He'll stop you if it's wrong.

God gave others more special gifts than you. He's not fair. If He loved you He would give you better gifts. Tell God which gifts you want. Test Him. If He loves you He'll give you your heart's desire. If He doesn't, then He doesn't really love you. Maybe you're not really a Christian.

If you had a better job you'd make more money. If you made more money you could give more money to your church and foreign missions. You deserve a better job. If God really loved you He'd help you get a better job. He obviously doesn't really care about you.

Cheating is wrong normally. But if you can get into graduate school think of how much more you could do for God. Besides, God forgives, and your motives are to help Him. If God really loved you, you would be smarter and not have to cheat to serve Him. It's His fault you're not doing better in your classes. Grades come easy for others. He loves them more than you.

Silly? Maybe to some. But this type of attack goes on routinely and daily in the minds of many sincere Christians. Some are in your church. Doubts of God's goodness and fear that He is maliciously holding back His best for them are constantly nagging them. The combination of Satan's solicitations and propositions from a world system in rebellion against God can become a formidable challenge for even a mature Christian. With enemies so real and temptation often so alluring, why do we plan to sin? Isn't the challenge to overcome the world, the flesh and the devil great enough without deliberately planning out our sin and giving advantages to our spiritual enemies?

Spiritual Warfare with the World: A Biblical Solution.

Let's review for a minute. What is the world in this context? The world is an organized system in rebellion against God. What makes up the world? The world is made up of the lust of the flesh, the lust of the eyes and the boastful pride of life.

Is there an easy way to remember how to explain the lust of the flesh, the lust of the eyes and the boastful pride of life? Yes. The lust of the flesh is another way of describing external propositions designed to stimulate physiological urges. The lust of the eyes is a Biblical way of describing our battle with feelings that we have to obtain beautiful things to be content or significant. The best description of the boastful pride of life is selfish ambition.

Christians in John's day had to deal with all three of the struggles making up the world system. Two thousand years later we are still fighting the same battles. The exact circumstances may have changed, but the realities of the battle have not. Lurid ads and billboards, keeping up with the Jones and personal plans that exclude God are as common now as they were two thousand years ago. Little appears to have really changed.

The challenges involved with the world are complex. How are we, as Christians, supposed to Biblically respond to the world's propositions? The same three verses of 1 John we read earlier reveal the solution for effectively overcoming the world. Reread 1 John 2:15–17.

Do not love the world, nor the things in the world. If
anyone loves the world, the love of the Father is not
in him. For all that is in the world, the lust of the
flesh and the lust of the eyes and the boastful pride
of life, is not from the Father, but is from the world.
And the world is passing away, and also its lusts;
but the one who does the will of God abides forever.
1 John 2:15–17

What is the Biblical solution to the challenges spelled out
in these verses? Look carefully at verse 17.

And the world is passing away, and also its lusts;
but the one who does the will of God abides forever.

One word contains the key to successfully dealing with the
world's propositions to sin. That word is "EVALUATE." I
constantly get propositioned to exchange eternally valuable things
for temporal things that are fading away. Do I really want to
exchange more value for less? If I do, I've just made a foolish
trade.

I'll never forget a lesson I learned as a small child when
one of my brothers asked me to trade him my small dime for his
large nickel. Trusting my brother, and unaware of the difference in
the values of the two coins, I agreed. I guess I assumed that if his
nickel was bigger and shinier than my dirty dime, it was worth
more, too. Bigger is better, right?

I ran over to our oldest brother and told him about my
trading adventure. He broke the news to me and explained that I
needed to get my dime back. I don't remember if I got it back or
not, but I do remember being confused and thinking that my own
brother had betrayed me.

What's the point? If I was naive and foolish enough to
trade my brother a dime for a nickel, how are people going to feel
trading eternal life for seventy years? Jesus called the rich farmer a
fool for being wealthy by worldly standards, but spiritually
bankrupt from God's perspective.

In John 3:36 Jesus said that those who believe in Him will receive eternal life, but those who refuse to do so will have the wrath of God abiding upon them forever. What do you say to someone who willingly trades away the opportunity to have eternal life with God for the temporary trash of this world—a decision that will ultimately result in that person being eternally separated from the love and presence of God? Talk about a naive and foolish trade.

What could be worse? How many men, women and children are trading away eternal treasure for earthly junk? The big, shiny nickel looks so much more valuable than the small, dirty dime. But the dime is worth twice as much. The fading value of earthly treasure can look really good for a time. But eternity will show its true value. How much more is eternity worth than seventy years?

The lust of the flesh, the lust of the eyes and the boastful pride of life are fading away. But the things of God will abide forever. How important is it to refuse to sell out cheap, no matter how alluring the world's temporal proposition appears? The relevant question is not whether or not the things of this world can look good, but whether or not they are worth the price tag that goes along with them.

To trade spending an eternity with God in heaven for an eternity in hell just for bigger barns is more than a poor trade, it is tragically and eternally stupid. But millions of men and women make that trade every day believing that Earth's treasures and the applause of man are more important than heaven's glory and the applause of God. This world is filled with just as many naive and foolish adults as it is children. Their tinsel and toys may be more expensive, but the results are still the same.

In contrasting eternal and temporal values, have you ever seriously pondered the notion that, according to the Bible, all of the decisions of Christians planted on the foundation of Jesus Christ ultimately have eternal consequences? Take a minute and reread 1 Corinthians 3:10–15.

According to the grace of God which was given to me, as a wise master builder I laid a foundation and another is building upon it. But let each man be careful how he builds upon it. For no man can lay a foundation other than the one which is laid, which is Jesus Christ. Now if any man builds upon the foundation with gold, silver, precious stones, wood, hay, straw, each man's work will become evident; for the day will show it, because it is to be revealed with fire; and the fire itself will test the quality of each man's work. If any man's work which he has built upon it remains, he shall receive a reward. If any man's work is burned up, he shall suffer loss; but he himself shall be saved, yet so as through fire.

In a real sense every Christian is in the construction business. According to these verses the fact that we are all building on the foundation of Christ is not optional. Apparently the only option we have is what kinds of materials will represent our words, thoughts and deeds.

Every decision we make as Christians will ultimately be viewed as valuable, (gold, silver and precious stones) or worthless, (wood, hay and straw). Either our decisions honor Christ or they do not. It would be more comfortable if God's Word taught that there are three types of materials we can use to build on our foundation of Christ. Some decisions represent valuable work, some represent worthless work, and some represent work that is less than valuable, but not totally worthless. Kind of a "C" grade on a standard bell curve.

The problem with having a third option is that God has not given us that choice. The New Testament clearly deems choices either valuable or worthless. Either you have the Son or you do not. The road is narrow or it is broad. The water is sweet or salty. The fruit is good or bad. The tree is either a good tree or a bad one.

Because our culture and age assume personal choices as entitlements rather than privileges, God's judgment of the value of our works may seem harsh and restrictive. But He is the one who makes the rules, as difficult as that is for some to accept.

According to God, truth is not relative, and it does not depend upon popularity polls of people whose foundation is moral and ethical relativism. We may chafe at God's authority, but that does not change it.

God promises believers that He will reward valuable work for eternity. *If any man's work which he has built upon it remains, he shall receive a reward.* It is just as clear that He will burn worthless work to ashes and forfeit potential eternal rewards. *If any man's work is burned up, he shall suffer loss; but he himself shall be saved, yet so as through fire.* Note carefully that a person's eternal salvation is not at stake here, only his or her opportunity to receive eternal rewards for faithful service. *But he himself shall be saved; yet so as through fire.*

> *Don't worry Karl, if hell is real and I go there, at least I'll be with all my friends. I'm going to live hard, die young and make a good-looking corpse. I'm going in style and having fun doing it. Ha ha ha!*

Do you think that's a funny line? I don't. But millions of people seem to think it makes sense. If I stood on a corner and gave away hundred dollar bills for one dollar someone would pull me aside for my own good and tell me to quit giving others such a good deal. If I continued this practice for long, someone would lock me up in a safe place.

> *Are you crazy? You just can't go on giving up more for less.*

But let someone consistently warn others that giving up heaven for hell is a fool's trade and see who is called crazy. Perspective is important.

> *Make your mark now. Don't get too religious or you may lose business contacts.*

> *Don't let them know you're a Christian. Grades are important if you want to get into graduate school. Blow this opportunity and you'll never get a second chance.*

Compared to other girls you come off like Mother Teresa. Do you want to date or not? Loosen up a little. Have some fun. It's okay. No one will ever know anyway. This is the twenty-first century. Who cares what other people think!

The government already robs honest people blind. So what if you hedge on your taxes some? Everybody does it. If your conscience bothers you, donate some of what you get to the poor.

The bottom line is that some things are temporal and some are eternal in value. The results of some of our decisions will produce eternal rewards and others will not. Is it possible to tell the difference between these two types of decisions? Yes it is. The key to consistent victory over a world system in rebellion against God is to consciously and consistently evaluate the world's temporary propositions through the grid of God's eternal Word, the Bible.

A good question to ask when you must sort through a worldly proposition is: *Is this a good decision from the perspective of time and eternity or just for time?* If it's good from the eternal perspective, then I'm free to say "yes." If it's not a good choice from the perspectives of both time and eternity, then I'm just as free to say "no," I won't buy the lie nor will I agree to sell out cheap. I'm not for sale.

Question: If you don't know what God's perspective is on a given choice, what decision do you make? Evaluating propositions from God's eternal perspective assumes we know His perspective on that subject. God has clearly revealed His will for mankind in His inerrant Word, the Bible. If we don't study God's Word (2 Timothy 2:15) and walk controlled by the Holy Spirit (Galatians 5:16), how are we going to evaluate the source and value of the propositions we face in an intelligent, effective manner? Jesus told His disciples in John 8:32:

You shall know the truth and the truth will set you free.

Of course He was right. How often do we have to be reminded to read our Bibles, even as sincere Christians? Light dispels darkness, and truth exposes falsehood. But we must know the truth to discern the difference. It's politically correct today to say that it's not possible to know absolute truth. (Relativists are absolutely certain this is true.)

Jesus, however, disagreed with this lie, too. He declared that God's Word is truth (John 17:17) and that He was truth incarnated (John 1:14, 14:6).

How important is it to know Jesus as our Savior? How important is it to study and understand God's Word? How important is it for a Christian to have consistent victory over the world?

How can a person consistently evaluate this world's propositions and say no to its lies, if he does not recognize the truth? How important is it to be Biblically correct in light of eternity, even if it means being considered politically incorrect for a time?

Christians who desire to consistently win more battles than they lose are individuals who know the truth and are capable of evaluating the world's lies against that truth. Public opinion changes by the day. God's Word will not change. Choosing between being politically correct and Biblically correct isn't a difficult choice for the Christian concerned about God's eternal perspective. What is the key to consistent victory over this world system? EVALUATE the proposition and say yes to the eternal perspective. Christian, are you courageous enough to consistently refuse to trade God's dimes for this world's nickels? Whose opinion ultimately controls your daily decisions?

Remember, if someone tells you that the world can't look appealing, that is a lie. If the world didn't appear valuable, it wouldn't be the major problem it represents, even for sincere Christians. The issue isn't whether the world has tinsel and trappings to offer for our allegiance, the real question is whether or not the price tag that goes along with selling out for temporal treasure is worth the cost. From Old Testament examples to New Testament commands, the answer is the same. Giving up eternal treasure for temporary trinkets is not worth the cost of the price tag.

In Matthew 6:24 and James 4:4, Jesus and His half-brother James essentially respond to questions regarding our professed love for God and our involvement in a world system that is in active rebellion against Him in the same way.

> *No one can serve two masters; for either he will hate the one and love the other, or he will hold to one and despise the other. You cannot serve God and mammon.*

> *You adulteresses do you not know that friendship with the world is hostility toward God? Therefore whoever wishes to be a friend of the world makes himself an enemy of God.*

In summary, the Bible calls the first piece of the spiritual warfare pie we must learn to recognize and contend with the world. We can choose to win in this conflict on a consistent basis by applying God's solution to this problem or we can choose to lose these same battles by ignoring His directives and relying on sincerity and luck. Most Christians already lose enough battles without planning to fail. Enough said, let's move on to the second piece of the spiritual warfare pie.

5

The Flesh:

Internal Solicitation to Sin

But I say, walk by the Spirit, and you will not carry out the desire of the flesh. For the flesh sets its desire against the Spirit, and the Spirit against the flesh; for these are in opposition to one another, so that you may not do the things that you please.
Galatians 5:16–17

That which I am doing, I do not understand; for I am not practicing what I would like to do, but I am doing the very thing I hate. But if I do the very thing I do not wish to do, I agree with the Law, confessing that it is good. So now, no longer am I the one doing it, but sin which indwells me. For I know that nothing good dwells in me, that is, in my flesh; for the wishing is present in me, but the doing of the good is not. For the good that I wish, I do not do; but I practice the very evil that I do not wish. But if I am doing the very thing I do not wish, I am no longer the one doing it, but sin which dwells in me. I find then the principle that evil is present in me, the one who wishes to do good. For I joyfully concur with the law of God in the inner man, but I

> *see a different law in the members of my body,*
> *waging war against the law of my mind, and making*
> *me a prisoner of the law of sin which is in my*
> *members. Wretched man that I am! Who will set me*
> *free from the body of this death? Thanks be to God*
> *through Jesus Christ our Lord! So then, on the one*
> *hand I myself with my mind am serving the law of*
> *God, but on the other, with my flesh the law of sin.*
> Romans 7:15–25

Our battle with the flesh is real, as noted in Galatians 5 and Romans 7, and it represents the second spiritual warfare opponent examined in this study. Just in case someone assumes this struggle with the flesh represents a problem for only the young or the spiritually immature but not for the mature Christian, remember who wrote these words and to whom he wrote.

The Apostle Paul was dedicated, sincere and spiritually mature. In spite of his commitment and dedication as an Apostle, he clearly still struggled with the flesh. Both passages cited are admonitions to Christians. When fleshly battles seem particularly discouraging, it might not hurt to remember the company we find contending with these same issues in the New Testament. Some may casually dismiss the flesh, but Scripture and experience testify that it will not depart from anyone this side of glory.

The *flesh* represents one third of the threefold opposition Christians must learn to confront and overcome if we desire to live victoriously as ambassadors for Christ. The *world* and the *devil* complete this contentious triad. We should not exaggerate or minimize the reality of the flesh as an active and aggressive opponent within each Christian. Blaming the flesh or old nature for all of our problems is just as irresponsible as deliberately ignoring or denying its existence.

Successful spiritual warfare demands a balanced approach to daily living and its conflicts. To function as salt and light in this crooked world, we must take each enemy seriously. Balance is a terrific concept, but, pragmatically speaking, it is often difficult to achieve, much less to consistently maintain.

Private agendas, fear and excuses make it easy to focus on one area of spiritual opposition (the world, the flesh or the devil) at the expense of the others. We need to check all three opponents regularly because each can seriously trouble a Christian. But the believer who is walking in obedience to the Holy Spirit can effectively overcome all of them

Winning athletes realize the importance of developing all of the major muscle groups necessary to excel in their given sport. A pitcher who has a powerful arm but weak legs will not pitch in the major leagues. A football player who has worked hard at developing his lower body strength but ignored building his upper body and back will spend more time sitting on the bench than playing on the field.

Effective weight training programs systematically work the legs, the back *and* the upper body. A person may not work each muscle group every day, or even on the same day. But he must work every muscle group if he hopes to be adequately equipped for serious action.

Christians that focus on the flesh at the expense of the world and the devil, or on the devil at the expense of the world and the flesh, etc., are as shortsighted as athletes who develop one muscle group while ignoring others. Since all three enemies are real, we need to make sure we are ready to deal with each one if we seriously hope to win more battles than we lose. The challenge before us is not just learning to identify the source of our conflict, but also understanding how to consistently overcome it by the grace and power of God.

Let's take a minute to address a potentially puzzling question regarding the flesh. What is the difference between the flesh as outlined in Romans 7 and Galatians 5 and the *lust* of the flesh described as part of the "world" system in 1 John 2: 15–17?

There is a major difference between the two, and the answer to this question is not as complicated as one might think.

The *lust* of the flesh, in the context of the "world" described in 1 John, represents external propositions intended to stimulate or control physiological urges. Pictures of scantily dressed individuals selling health club memberships or intimate apparel would qualify. A billboard advertisement of a bowl of ice cream, a lobster dripping in butter or a medium rare steak could work as well.

In contrast to the *external* propositions of the world system, Romans 7:15–25 and Galatians 5:16–17 clearly identify the flesh as an *internal* struggle waging war within us and against us. Recognizing the source of the proposition as either internal or external is the key to discerning whether the immediate source of battle with the flesh is from the world or from our inherited sinful nature.

Reread Romans 7:15–25 and Galatians 5:17.

*That which I am doing, I do not understand; for I am not practicing what I would like to do, but I am doing the very thing I hate. But if I do the very thing I do not wish to do, I agree with the Law, confessing that it is good. So now, no longer am I the one doing it, **but sin which indwells me**. For I know that nothing good dwells in me, that is, in my flesh; for the wishing is present in me, but the doing of the good is not. For the good that I wish, I do not do; but I practice the very evil that I do not wish. **But if I am doing the very thing I do not wish, I am no longer the one doing it, but sin which dwells in me. I find then the principle that evil is present in me, the one who wishes to do good**. For I joyfully concur with the law of God in the inner man, but **I see a different law in the members of my body, waging war against the law of my mind, and making me a prisoner of the law of sin which is in my members.** Wretched man that I am! Who will set*

*me free from the body of this death? Thanks be to
God through Jesus Christ our Lord! So then, on the
one hand I myself with my mind am serving the law
of God, but on the other, with my flesh the law of
sin.* Romans 7:15–25

*For the flesh sets its desire against the Spirit, and
the Spirit against the flesh; for these are in
opposition to one another, so that you may not do
the things that you please.* Galatians 5:17

Most Christians will readily admit that the realities of the
internal struggles described in both Romans and Galatians are all
too familiar. Although new life in Christ does mean that we are no
longer legally slaves of sin, dominated and controlled by fleshly
desires, it does not guarantee freedom from daily struggles. As
soldiers of Christ our promise is victory in battle, not the absence
of conflict.

Salvation in Christ provides believers with a choice. We
can now choose to let either the flesh or the Spirit control us.
Before our conversion we had no choice in the matter: *But a
natural man does not accept the things of the Spirit of God; for
they are foolishness to him, and he cannot understand them,
because they are spiritually appraised.* 1 Corinthians 2:14

As believers in the Lord Jesus Christ, we now have a
choice:

*Do not be deceived, God is not mocked; for
whatever a man sows, this he will also reap. For the
one who sows to his own flesh shall from the flesh
reap corruption, but the one who sows to the Spirit
shall from the Spirit reap eternal life.* Galatians
6:7–8

Galatians 5:19–21 indicates the evidence of a believer's life
controlled by the flesh:

*Now the deeds of the flesh are evident, which are:
immorality, impurity, sensuality, idolatry, sorcery,
enmities, strife, jealousy, outbursts of anger,*

disputes, dissensions, factions, envying, drunkenness, carousing, and things like these, of which I forewarned you just as I have forewarned you that those who practice such things shall not inherit the kingdom of God.

Galatians 5:22–23 describes the results of a Christian life yielded to and controlled by the Spirit:

But the fruit of the Spirit is love, joy, peace, patience, kindness, goodness, faithfulness, gentleness, self-control; against such things there is no law.

I thought that as a Christian I was done with selfishness and exploiting others. Is there something wrong with me that I still have selfish, self-serving thoughts and desires? No, because facing conflicting choices is not the problem. That is a privilege. The issue is the choice I make. I can now choose to serve Christ or myself. I am legally free from the curse and dominion of sin to choose whom I will serve.

Attempts to relegate daily battles with the flesh to passive struggles from habits and former memories are simply not credible Biblically or experientially. Freedom in Christ does not change the fact that even Spirit-controlled believers still live with an active traitor inside.

Galatians 5:16 clearly articulates the good news for Christians concerning this interior struggle. When we walk controlled by the Holy Spirit, the strong desires of our flesh will not dominate our thinking or actions.

Theoretically, Christians may claim victory over the flesh moment by moment, day by day. But the pragmatic truth remains that the flesh is a constant enemy and an active challenge for the believer until the Lord changes our corrupted body into an incorruptible one.

As I gain insight into God's character and perspective on any given subject, I grow in my capacity to make wise decisions. The more familiar I am with Scripture, the easier it is to identify temptations. I can say "Yes" to the truths of God and "No" to the lies of our opposition. Truth sets people free. But we cannot choose truth if we do not recognize it. Therefore, we must invest our time in studying the Bible because we know it is true and indispensable for making evaluations that consistently honor God.

Before we move on to tackle the flesh, take a minute and review several key ideas from the previous chapter that help us to identify and successfully deal with the world.

In dealing with the "world," we learned that we must "evaluate" in order to find the key to consistent victory. The world tries to proposition us to trade our eternal reward and treasure for the fleeting pleasures of time here and now.

Whether that temptation comes through the lust of the flesh, the lust of the eyes or the boastful pride of life, the principle remains the same. We must evaluate each solicitation and say "No" to the things of time and the world and "Yes" to the eternal things of God. Trading dimes for nickels is foolish, in spite of the fact that the nickel is larger.

If warfare simply required just one generic prayer that covered the fight against all three enemies, the Christian life would indeed be easier. Unfortunately, warfare does not work that way. In 2 Timothy 2:15 God commands us to study to show ourselves approved as workmen who have learned to rightly divide the word of truth. Though there are a number of good reasons to obey this command, one is the certainty of facing spiritual warfare.

Evaluating worldly propositions through the grid of Scripture, and saying "Yes" to God's eternal perspective regardless of politically correct confusion, is the believer's key to victory over the world. But according to Scripture, we handle our battles with the flesh in an entirely different manner.

Although this may seem confusing at first, Christians discover the Scriptural truth that the Lord provides His children with an effective defense for any fleshly scenario we face. If we respond to the flesh differently than how we respond to the world, then how *are* we to respond to active opposition from the flesh?

According to the Bible, there are at least three different ways Christians can overcome this second area of the spiritual conflict. We are instructed to *run* (2 Timothy 2:22), to *renew our minds* (Ephesians 4:22–24), *and to walk controlled by or filled by the Spirit* (Galatians 5:16, Ephesians 5:17–18).

1.   Run

Now flee from youthful lusts, and pursue righteousness, faith, love, and peace, with those who call on the Lord from a pure heart. 2 Timothy 2:22

Youthfulness is not a Biblical excuse for sensuality, immorality, roller coaster faith, conditional love or rebellion. Apparently, in dealing with the flesh, there are some issues that are so hot that the best response is to simply run. Someone may object that a victorious Christian shouldn't have to run from any opposition for doesn't Romans 8 declare that we are more than conquerors in Christ Jesus? Why would a conqueror run?

It is true that in Christ we are more than conquerors. But a wise soldier, seasoned in battle, lives to fight another day while a naive, green soldier is much more likely to become a statistical casualty. After all, as Solomon said, *better a living dog than a dead lion* (Ecclesiastes 9:4).

Do you remember the story about Joseph and Potifer's wife in Genesis 39? While Potifer was away, his wife propositioned Joseph with lurid sexual advances. Did Joseph stand around and evaluate her appeals for sex? Did he think, *I need to take a few minutes and evaluate her propositions?*

When she reached for his clothes, he reached for the door and ran as fast as he could. Was his response to run that of a defeated, shameful coward? Or was it the wise, courageous response of a godly young man who didn't want to play with fire? Some temptations are just too hot for a mindful response and necessitate a hasty retreat.

In his excellent book *Counter Attack*, Jay Carty offers several chapters that deal with the common struggles Christians often have with the flesh. In a chapter focused on overeating, he suggests avoiding the donut shop altogether so as to prevent the sin of eating too many chocolate éclairs. Simple? Yes. Running from a problem? In an intelligent way, yes. Effective? Sure. Pragmatically speaking, does it work? Absolutely!

Jay goes on to humorously illustrate many of the needless temptations we Christians face on a daily basis, such as when we go into a store and buy chocolate éclairs, promising that we will only look at them in the refrigerator. The example makes us laugh even while we recognize that it is pathetic and tragic. Driving home a different way to avoid the donut shop is a wise choice for someone serious about avoiding this particular temptation. This begs the question, but is this the response of a cowardly soldier or an intelligent warrior?

When we face personally difficult temptations, Scripture teaches us to simply walk or literally run away from the temptation. Pornography is a multibillion dollar industry in our country. Christians are not immune to this consuming, degrading and exploitive problem. Just ask the pastor of any large church. Sometimes wisdom and common sense scream, "Run!" Don't sit there and evaluate the situation. Lace up your running shoes and hit the road. If you have to drive home a different way, then do it— even if it means taking an extra twenty minutes. A clean conscience is worth more than the cost of a little extra gas. Solomon asked, *can a man play with fire and not get burned?* The answer is "No."

2.   Renew your mind

I urge you therefore, brethren, by the mercies of God to present your bodies a living and holy sacrifice, acceptable to God, which is your spiritual service of worship. And do not be conformed to this world, but be transformed by the renewing of your mind, that you may prove what the will of God is, that which is good and acceptable and perfect.
Romans 12:1–2

> *...that, in reference to your former manner of life,*
> *you lay aside the old self, which is being corrupted*
> *in accordance with the lusts of deceit, and that you*
> *be renewed in the spirit of your mind, and put on*
> *the new self, which in the likeness of God has been*
> *created in righteousness and holiness of the truth.*
> Ephesians 4:22–24

A second defensive response to the lust of the flesh that God provides for His children focuses on the renewing of our mind. When we choose to win in our mind, we will win in life. When we choose to lose in our mind, it is only a matter of time before we lose those battles in our lives. Compromise *always* begins in our mind. Typically, the longer we think about a particular action, the easier it is to rationalize it.

How many outbursts of anger erupt from an empty vacuum? Volcanic eruptions occur when the lid holding down the top is no longer heavy enough to contain the pressure. The result is an explosion.

Likewise, most explosions of anger occur after our thoughts and imaginary conversations reach a boiling point. At some point, a verbal eruption explodes from our lips. To the bystander the outburst looks spontaneous. But those close to the source of the eruption can predict the overflow of unresolved bitterness, pent up thoughts and unfinished conversations that need resolution.

How many men or women do you suppose participate in sexually immoral activities without first thinking about their actions long enough to make them seem like a reasonable option? When someone seeks help with sexual sin from me and begins by saying he doesn't know how or why it happens, should I automatically assume he's telling me the truth? That the offense occurred may be true. But that it suddenly sprang from a pure heart and mind is a lie. If I ask him about his daydreams, and he is honest, I can depend on his dreaming about sexual fantasies. I can also depend on his using some type of pornography and sexual self-gratification and accurately guess that these fantasies consume much of his attention and routine.

Where was this, or any, battle first lost? Does it begin in the bed or in the head?

When I choose to win battles with the flesh in my mind, *I do not have to lose those battles in life*. When I allow myself to lose these battles in my mind, it is only a matter of time before I lose these battles in my life. What is in our minds eventually controls us.

Proverbs 23:7 declares: *For as he thinks within himself, so he is*. When the flesh consumes my mind and heart, the results are predictable.

The results are also predictable with the tables turned. When I fill my mind with thinking upon that which honors God, my life reflects that honor. Godly actions do not occur in an empty vacuum, and neither do godless ones

If renewing our minds is an essential key to victory over the flesh, how is it done? Once again, I am indebted to Jay Carty and his book *Counter Attack* for the basic concepts that follow on substitutive thinking. The process is both simple and effective.

Pink elephants and white polar bears

Imagine a pink elephant. If you look closely you can see it has three red socks and a blue one. On its trunk is a green muffler. Can you see it? Its ears are flapping back and forth very rhythmically. On its forehead a neon light is flashing the name "Dumbo" in time with its flowing, flapping ears. Got it?

Now I want you to completely forget about that pink elephant. Stop thinking about its three red socks and green muffler. And whatever you do don't imagine that flashing sign blinking in time with his flapping ears. Stop, stop, stop thinking about that pink elephant.

What do you do every time I tell you to quit thinking about it? You see a pink elephant complete with socks, muffler and neon sign, right? Now I want you to imagine a white polar bear. He's fishing for salmon, sitting on a white iceberg and dipping his paw in the water trying to scoop up a fish. His nose and paw pads are black. Everything else is white except the salmon he has caught, which is flopping around on the iceberg. Can you see the white polar bear and the salmon? Of course you can.

Are you still actively thinking about a pink elephant? No. You are focused on the polar bear and flopping fish. So what's the point? Pink elephants represent thoughts we don't want to think about while white polar bears represent the things we want to dwell on. Usually whatever we think on long and hard is what we end up trying to reproduce in life.

Think through Proverbs 23:7 one more time. "As a man thinks within himself, so is he." What does this have to do with substitutive thinking? For too long we have approached our struggles with the world and the flesh by saying "No, don't." "I won't lust, I won't get angry, I won't be bitter; I won't, I won't, I won't." If lust, anger and bitterness represent the pink elephants I need to leave behind, what happens every time I say "I won't?" I simply reinforce the very thoughts I am trying to put behind.

Saying "No" to pink elephants is a good first step to victory, but it isn't enough. Besides saying "No" to wrong thinking, we must also say "Yes" to right thinking. It's one thing to admit we have sinned. It's another matter to agree with God that His way is right and that we must do things His way. When we learn to win in our head we will win in life. When we allow ourselves to lose in our thought lives, it is just a matter of time before we lose in life. Why? Because we typically rationalize the things we choose to think on long and hard.

If I struggle with anger (a pink elephant), I need a white polar bear to replace the pink elephant I am struggling with in my mind. James 1:19–20 says that I am to be "quick to hear, slow to speak, and slow to anger." Why? "Because the anger of man will not accomplish the righteousness of God." I have two ears and one mouth—a pretty good visual aid when I get up each morning and stare at what just crawled out of bed. Listen twice as much as you talk.

When someone says or does something that hurts and I feel like getting angry, at that very moment I want to remember, "Be quick to hear, slow to speak, slow to become angry." Why? Because the more I talk, in all likelihood, the worse things are going to get. By purposely concentrating on a white polar bear I am able to respond by refocusing on what I want to think about rather than react by focusing on the type of thinking that usually reinforces my pink elephants and escalates the potential problem.

By substituting what I want to think about for the things I need to put behind me, I learn to win in my head. With practice the white polar bears can become as normal a thought pattern as the pink elephants currently are. It is possible to make a game out of finding white polar bears to substitute for the fleshly thoughts, which, left unchallenged, will slowly control my mind and rob my joy.

Examples of helpful white polar bear verses might include James 1:19–20, which deals with anger; Ephesians 4:29, which addresses a smart mouth; Philippians 4:8, which addresses lust; and Ephesians 4:31–32 for problems with bitterness, wrath, anger and slander. There is really no limit to the number of verses applicable as white polar bear substitutions. Actually, the more creative a person becomes in this exercise the better. The ultimate object is to consciously refocus our thinking on what we should accept rather than on what we need to reject. Sometimes we remember unique verses or ideas more easily than familiar ones.

But remember, we do not have to limit polar bear substitutions to just Scripture verses. Several years ago one of our church members told me that her polar bear substitution was immediate prayer for family members who were not yet Christians. The method may differ, but the principle is exactly the same. We learn to substitute things we want to think on deeply for the things we know we should not allow to consume our minds and time.

By consistently choosing to control our thinking rather than allowing it to control us, we can respond immediately and Biblically to temptation rather than becoming caught up once again in a frustrating cycle of react, regret, repeat and remorse.

Have you ever watched someone shoot a pistol? At a distance it looks like the person points the gun and it just goes off. In reality, several mechanical actions occur before the person actually fires the shot. He feeds the shell into the firing chamber, cocks the hammer and squeezes the trigger. The hammer falls, the firing pin explodes the cartridge in the chamber, and finally the bullet flies out the barrel towards a target.

Things happen so quickly that even though many separate actions actually occur, they appear as one continuous action. Learning to substitute white polar bears for pink elephants may feel mechanical at first. But like most good or bad habits, they become routine through practice. Like shooting a gun, after a while the substitutive thinking can become so automatic that it appears as one fluid response. Point and shoot, automatic. Pink elephants to white polar bears, automatic. If developing a good habit takes some time, that's okay. Each day I am learning to confront temptations while they are still in my mind rather than wait until the deed is done and the damage is greater for everyone touched by the problem.

If the troubling issue is a problem of the flesh and not demonic, this profoundly simple game will work in helping a person take every thought captive to Christ. If the problem is demonic in nature rather than just fleshly, pink elephants and white polar bears won't eliminate the actual source of the problem.

If we can fix a car by putting gas in the tank, it is a lot cheaper to do that than paying a mechanic to tear the engine apart. In the same way, it makes sense in warfare counseling to begin by checking the most obvious alternatives first. Win in your mind and you will win in your life. Lose in your mind and you will lose in your life. The issue may have far more to do with a volitional choice of allowing my mind to control me than it has to do with a demon potentially controlling my mind.

3.   Walk controlled by the Holy Spirit

The filling of the Holy Spirit is a subject that many have neglected, abused and often ignored. Among some Christians, there seems more proactive discussion and specific indoctrination regarding the filling and baptism of the Holy Spirit than about sharing the saving Gospel of the Lord Jesus Christ. Among other Christians, the third member of the Trinity could probably go on vacation and never be missed. According to Galatians 5:16, walking under the control of the Holy Spirit is the key to consistent victory over the flesh.

What does being controlled by the Holy Spirit mean, and how can I do it?

Many books exist on this topic. Some are helpful, others are not. It is possible to make this issue so divisive or confusing that it is easier to avoid the subject than risk offending egos and damaging relationships. Understanding the filling and controlling of the Holy Spirit is so vitally necessary for victory over the flesh though that we cannot afford the luxury of skipping it.

Good teachers and trainers have the ability and responsibility to take complex materials and communicate them in a clear, concise fashion. The end of good teaching is not simply dumping accurate data, but rather equipping fellow members of the body to thoroughly understand and confidently apply the things they have learned to their daily circumstances.

We must not allow teaching on a topic as important as the filling of the Holy Spirit to turn into a subjective, confusing excuse for men and women to judge the sincerity and spirituality of other Christians. When we allow this to happen, it dishonors God and cheats His true church. As the world we live in seems to be less and less a place we can call home, it is more important than ever that God's church has clear, Biblical, transferable instruction available.

What does it mean to walk controlled by the Holy Spirit? Galatians 5:16 commands Christians to walk controlled by the Holy Spirit. Ephesians 5:18 commands believers to be filled with the Holy Spirit. The principles and results are the same. The word "fill" means "to control." To be filled with the Holy Spirit is to be controlled by the Spirit, and to be controlled by the Holy Spirit is to be filled by Him.

> *But I say, walk by the Spirit, and you will not carry out the desire of the flesh.* Galatians 5:16

> *And do not get drunk with wine, for that is dissipation, but be filled with the Spirit, ... "* Ephesians 5:18

Word pictures sometimes explain a word's meaning. One popular word picture many people use to explain the meaning of the word "fill" is a sailboat. As the wind fills the sail it is possible to control the boat's direction. A windless day cannot empower or control a sailboat. But once the wind hits the sail both are possible. When believers choose to confess any known sins between themselves and God, and yield total control of their entire lives to God, they are free to ask God the Holy Spirit to supernaturally fill, control and empower them to serve Christ, and subsequently they have the ability to consistently walk in victory over the flesh.

The keys to consistent victory over the flesh can involve 1) running—too hot, 2) renewing—victory begins in the mind, and 3) walking controlled by the Holy Spirit—a believer's supernatural resource for victorious Christian living on a daily basis.

The good news is this. Victory over the flesh is not only possible for a growing Christian, we should consider it normal. How we respond depends upon the nature of the particular solicitation in question. Sometimes the issue is just too hot and the righteous response is to just run. Other issues are not too hot; they just involve a decision to submit each thought captive to Christ, remembering victory over sin begins in our mind. Lastly, victory over the flesh is guaranteed when we walk controlled and empowered by the Holy Spirit.

The point to remember? Although all three of these possible responses are effective ways to deal with the flesh, Scripture does not prescribe any of the three as a response to temptation and solicitation from the world. If a Christian has not learned how to recognize the source of the solicitation, then his subsequent response will be at best a guess, which does not lend itself to consistent victorious Christian living.

Understanding both areas of spiritual warfare is not just optional, it is non-negotiable for Christians who want to win more battles than they lose. Our responses are not generic; they are specific, depending upon the source of the temptation. So far so good.

We began our discussion on the spiritual warfare pie though by stating that it consists of three equal pieces. We have taken a brief look at two slices of this pie. It is now time to move on to the third piece, which is the devil or supernatural solicitation.

6

The Devil:

Supernatural Solicitation to Sin

Submit therefore to God. Resist the devil and he will flee from you. Draw near to God and He will draw near to you. Cleanse your hands, you sinners; and purify your hearts, you double-minded. Be miserable and mourn and weep; let your laughter be turned into mourning, and your joy to gloom. Humble yourselves in the presence of the Lord, and He will exalt you. James 4:7–10

Humble yourselves therefore, under the mighty hand of God, that He may exalt you at the proper time, casting all your anxiety upon Him, because He cares for you. Be of sober spirit, be on the alert. Your adversary, the devil, prowls about like a roaring lion, seeking someone to devour. But resist him firm in your faith, knowing that the same experiences of suffering are being accomplished by your brethren who are in the world. 1 Peter 5:6–9

Scripture makes it clear that demonic or supernatural spiritual warfare is real. It represents the third piece of the warfare pie that Christians must learn how to recognize and respond to if we hope to win more battles than we lose.

Accounts of demonic warfare did not seem to surprise or shock Jesus, the Apostles or the men and women to whom they ministered. Matthew, Luke, Paul, James, Peter, Jude and John each speak to the reality of satanic/demonic warfare (Matthew 4:1–12, Luke 10:17–20, Acts 5:1–5, 2 Corinthians 10:3–5, Ephesians 6:10–17, James 4:7–10, 1 Peter 5:6–9, Jude 8–9, and Revelation 12:10–11, respectively).

> *But whom you forgive anything, I forgive also; for indeed what I have forgiven, if I have forgiven anything, I did it for your sakes in the presence of Christ, in order that no advantage be taken of us by Satan; for we are not ignorant of his schemes.* 2 Corinthians 2:11

Apparently Paul felt confident reminding his readers that they were not ignorant of the "schemes" or methodologies of Satan regarding warfare. This may have been a reasonable assumption during Paul's day regarding those he personally ministered to, but I do not believe the church can honestly make the same claim today.

I have had Christian leaders—even pastors—tell me that they are not aware of ever having experienced demonic attacks in thirty, forty, fifty or even sixty years of service for Jesus Christ. I don't doubt the sincerity of the person who makes this type of statement, but I would challenge the comment's accuracy. My suspicion is that many Christians under the fiery attack of demonic archers have never learned how to recognize supernatural opposition. There always seems a more reasonable explanation than demons; and, when doubtful, they just blame the flesh or a weak will.

Although demons can attack Christians physically, they more typically focus their accusatory arrows against our minds. Why? As Proverbs 23:7 indicates, if you can control a person's thinking, you can ultimately control his actions. *For as he thinks within himself, so he is.* This type of attack is subtle and often more effective than creating an overt spectacle that could wake up even the sleepiest Christian from an apathetic stupor and motivate him to pick up his Bible and look for answers

What does demonic attack against Christians typically look like? Although I will answer this important question more completely later in this chapter, the bottom line is that the Christian mind is the primary battlefield of demonic attack. There is a direct correlation between the fiery arrows the Apostle Paul speaks of in Ephesians 6:16 and the debilitating accusation that the Apostle John references in Revelation 12:10.

> *...in addition to all, taking up the shield of faith with which you will be able to extinguish all the flaming missiles of the evil one.*

> *And I heard a loud voice in heaven, saying, "Now the salvation, and the power, and the kingdom of our God and the authority of His Christ have come, for the accuser of our brethren has been thrown down, who accuses them before our God day and night."*

What can this accusation sound like in the mind of a genuine Christian?

> *You are fat. You are ugly. No one likes you. Your prayers bounce off the ceiling, why do you bother praying anyway? You are a sexual pervert. You have committed the unforgivable sin. Read your Bible later; you are too sleepy to read right now. Why do you bother reading your Bible, you never get anything out of it anyway because you are not a true Christian. The Bible is not true. You are stupid. You are a hypocrite.*

It goes on and on, and no matter what you do, it is never enough. There is always something left undone, and some reason why you fail to measure up to God's expectations. As I mentioned earlier, a demon's first job is to keep you out of heaven. If he fails on that mission, his plan "B" is to keep you so preoccupied and distracted that you never feel qualified or have the time to help someone else get there.

How can a Christian tell the difference between demonic accusation, which we should ignore, and conviction from the Holy Spirit, which we should respond to immediately?

1   When the voice, the word, the idea or the impression whispered in your ear violates Scripture, it is not conviction from the Holy Spirit and you should ignore it.

Confess your sin again; you did not begin "our Father," and you forgot to end "in Jesus' name." Pray again with more sincerity so that God knows you mean it.

1 John 1:9 promises that when we confess our sins, God is faithful and just to forgive our sin and to cleanse us from all unrighteousness. The Bible nowhere teaches that we need to pray for others to show our sincerity and for God to forgive us. God would never whisper this into our ear, but a demon would.

2   When the voice, the word, the idea or the impression whispered in your ear is not specific but so general that you aren't even sure what you did wrong, it is not conviction from the Holy Spirit, and you should ignore it.

You feel depressed because you have sin in your life. Tell God you are sorry for disappointing Him and confess everything you have done wrong.

Part of the Holy Spirit's job is to convict us of sin so that we can get back to serving Jesus Christ. He is specific in His conviction and would never tease or torment us. A demon, on the other hand, takes great delight in teasing and tormenting us, hoping to keep us so preoccupied that we never feel free. There always seems something left undone that steals our joy and confidence in Christ.

3   When the voice, the word, the idea or the impression whispered in your ear is consistently demeaning and in second person pronoun, it is not the Holy Spirit's conviction, and you should ignore it.

You are fat, ugly and stupid. Things are never going to change. God does not listen to your prayers anyway. If God really loved you things would be different.

A demon is not going to speak to a Christian in a first person singular pronoun because it is not that person. But it will shoot its infernal arrows at him beginning with a second person singular pronoun. "You" this. "You" that. "You" always. "You" never, and so on. The truth is that we get so used to hearing the accusation and condemnation that we flip the pronouns from the second person to the first person. Slow down the tape and listen carefully; what you hear may surprise you. And if you happen to hear the accusatory voice communicating in a first person plural pronoun—"we"—it may be a clue that you are dealing with more than one demon. People don't speak to themselves in a first person plural pronoun: "We are fat," "we are ugly," "we are going to kill you," etc., but a demon speaking on behalf of more than one demon certainly might.

4   Pray offensively rather than defensively when the voice, the word, the idea or the impression whispered in your ear is accusatory rather than convicting.

Lord, if that is a demon telling me I am fat, ugly, stupid, a sexual pervert and a loser, and that You haven't forgiven my sin, please torment the one who is tormenting me, destroy the destroyer, undermine the one who is attempting right now to undermine me. Contend against the one that is contending against me and catch it in its own traps. Thank you! I pray this in the name of the Lord Jesus Christ.

God is willing and more than capable of protecting His children against demonic accusers. Psalm 27 is a good example of a defensive prayer asking God for protection. Psalm 35:1–8 is a good example of an offensive prayer asking God to destroy those who are attempting to destroy us. I have encouraged Christians for several decades to pray offensively. Ask God to unleash His power upon those attempting to destroy His children, just like King David did, and see what happens when those attacks are supernatural rather than natural.

If habitual feelings of unworthiness and condemnation are still mentally debilitating a person after consistently praying offensive prayers, the problem may be physiological or mental rather than demonic. It may also indicate the presence of a demon or demons holding ground 'topos' against that person—a problem we will explore in depth and learn how to resolve in this book. But if those feelings of unworthiness and condemnation leave as quickly as they arrived, welcome to the world of demonic warfare.

How should a Christian respond to demonic attack? Scripture is clear that Christians are to "resist" the devil and he will flee from us. Offensive prayer is resisting the devil. But to resist demonic attacks, we must first be able to recognize them for what they really are—lies from the pit of hell. We need to reject and ignore lies, not allow them to control our thinking and actions.

It would be much easier if all a Christian had to do was mumble one generic prayer to respond effectively to opposition from the world, the flesh and the devil. Kind of like rubbing a religious rabbit's foot. But Scripture is very clear that the spiritual opposition we face is made up of three different opponents, and our responses should be different, too.

For whatever the debatable reasons, it seems that many Christians today believe ignorance provides protection from demonic attack. As one sincere Christian Education leader told me, "Karl, if you study warfare they will get you." This dear Christian simply verbalized what others had told her and what many equally sincere Christians unfortunately still believe.

I thanked my friend for her genuine concern and requested her prayer support, but I also reminded her that fear is usually a very poor motivator for a Christian. Scripture clearly states that *perfect love casts out fear* and *greater is He who is in you than he who is in the world* (1 John 4:4, 18). The Apostle Paul reminded Christians that *God has not given us a spirit of timidity, but of power and love and discipline* (2 Timothy 1:7).

My experience counseling Christians involved in this type of conflict is that the more discerning and competent I have become in working with it, the less obvious and more subtle my battles have become. Truth sets people free (John 8:32). Standing on truth and the delegated authority of Jesus Christ is not an open invitation for demonic bondage. Quite the opposite. When demons realize that a Christian is no longer paralyzed through fear and that he can also shoot back, they hide behind trees rather than march in the open dressed in red coats. Demons are not stupid, and they do not enjoy divine retribution.

Let's dig a little deeper into this piece of the pie.

Oppression and possession

Oppression and *possession* are the two terms most commonly mentioned by Christian writers and speakers when referring to spiritual conflict with demonic spirits. They usually use the term *oppression* when referring to external spiritual harassment. It is quite normal in the life of a growing Christian, although there seems wide latitude in the intensity of this type of attack.

Possession is a word typically used to describe an internal condition experienced by non-Christians totally controlled and dominated by demonic spirits. It connotes the complete loss of self-control or self-will in contrast to the external darts of oppression Ephesians 6:16 refers to. It is not considered a normal condition even for non-Christians and is usually rejected as a possibility for genuine Christians.

C. Fred Dickason, a well known Biblical scholar and noted writer and speaker on the subject of demonic warfare, has clearly explained the historical elements and the development (etymology) of the two words *daimonizomai* and *daimonizomenos* used in the New Testament to describe varying degrees of demonic control experienced by human beings. In his classic book *Demon Possession & the Christian: A New Perspective,* Dr. Dickason has written:

> The verb *daimonizomai* means "to be possessed by a demon." The participle from the same root, *daimonizomenos*, is used twelve times in the Greek New Testament. It is used only in the present tense, indicating the continued state of one inhabited by a demon, or

demonized. This participle has components to its structure. First there is the root, *daimon*, which indicates the involvement of demons. Second is the causative stem, *iz*, which shows that there is an active cause in this verb. Third is the passive ending, *omenos*. This conveys the passivity of the person described as demonized.

Putting it all together, the participle in its root form means, "a demon caused passivity." This indicates a control other than that of the person who is demonized; he is regarded as the recipient of the demon's action. In other words, demonization pictures a demon controlling a somewhat passive human. (pg. 37)

Conversations on demonic warfare often use the word "ownership" in an attempt to distinguish between oppression and possession. Once again Dr. Dickason has provided a helpful clarification for this discussion.

Confusion has been introduced by translating this participle (daimonizomenos) as "demon possessed." The word possession implies ownership. Actually, demons own nothing. The New Testament regards them as squatters or invaders of territory that does not belong to them. In reality God owns them, for He is their Creator and their judge. Such a faulty translation, then, misleads people regarding the state of the demonized person and causes undue consternation and terror in the hearts of the afflicted and those concerned for him. (pg. 38)

As long as we accept conventional wisdom limiting a Christian's possible demonic conflict to simple external oppression and relegate possession to a positional problem that only a handful of non-Christians potentially face, we can feel fairly safe and secure in our assumptions regarding Christians and possible demonic conflict. The issue is clear, and the answer to this troubling question of possible demonic involvement for Christians is black and white. Non-Christians had better keep a sharp eye on how far they go with decisions that could possibly expose them to demonic involvement. But Christians are safe as long as they read their Bibles, confess their sins and faithfully pray the blood of Jesus. A problem for many concerned leaders is the fact that they regularly meet sincere Christians who read their Bibles (usually with great trouble and constant mental distractions), confess their sins (although their prayers never seem complete or sincere enough) and faithfully pray the blood of Jesus, who are still obviously troubled and wondering if the demeaning, accusatory haranguing they endure will ever end.

If we parrot the accepted conventional oppression/possession paradigm concerning spiritual warfare, what natural conclusions must we and the individual we are counseling draw? Either the person is a Christian with serious mental and/or emotional problems who needs "professional" long term counseling, or he is a weak-willed Christian who simply needs more discipline in his thinking and actions, or possibly he thinks he is a Christian but in fact is not. Pretty simple, so why all the fuss?

What do you say when the person being interviewed is as orthodox in his theology and as sincere and zealous in his dedication and devotion to Jesus Christ as you are, and yet his problems persist? What do you say after he has memorized Scripture and prayed consistently, and yet the daily mental accusations he endures continue to torment him, often to the point of contemplating suicide?

What trite answer should you give him? How much more guilt should we heap upon him? How much further should we push him into a performance trap that he can never win? Try as he may, this person's promises, prayers and performance never quite measure up. This type of individual is already under daily bombardment from mental anguish, bizarre inner thoughts and voices telling him:

> *You aren't good enough, you aren't really a Christian, no one in church really likes you, and Christian leaders are all hypocrites, so why listen to them? You aren't smart enough to study the Bible so why try? You're too tired to read your Bible and God doesn't hear your prayers, so why bother?*

You're fat, you're ugly, you're a failure and you
would do God a favor if you were dead. It's God's
will because at least then you would not confuse
others with your terrible testimony. You are a
terrible parent. You are a pathetic husband or wife.
You are a disappointment as a son or daughter. If
you promise to read your Bible more, then God
might still love you. If you pray more fervently, then
God may forgive and hear you. Things are never
going to change so give up and die.

What if our presuppositions concerning oppression and
possession are mistaken or at least incomplete? What if, like a
growing number of Evangelical leaders and counselors, we
challenge conventional wisdom and thinking on this subject rather
than the faith or sincerity of the person being counseled?
Ambiguity is frustrating, especially among spiritual leaders who
love God and teach others. But the fact is that well-known
Evangelical Bible teachers like John MacArthur and Charles
Swindoll have differing views on this particular issue. Both of
these men love God and are committed to consistent Bible study.
Their difference of opinion concerning the potential demonization
of true Christians ought to serve notice that we should approach
this subject with prayerful consideration rather than with
presuppositional dogmatism and arrogance.

There is a third category regarding possible spiritual
conflict that a growing number of Evangelical leaders and writers
have openly discussed. Men like the late Merrill Unger, Mark
Bubeck, Ed Murphy, Fred Dickason, Charles Swindoll and Neil
Anderson use terms like *demonization, invasion and infestation*
while speaking and writing about real demonic problems troubling
genuine believers. Their message, while including concerns about
the reality of oppression (fiery arrows) and possession (total
demonic domination and control), focuses on the degree of control
demons can exercise over Christians who are foolish enough to
willingly allow demonic spirits to gain control over areas of their
lives that the Holy Spirit should control. The Bible is clear that just
as the Holy Spirit can and should control a believer's life on a

daily basis (Ephesians 5:18), Christians can volitionally yield control of their lives to Satan and his demonic minions, a subject that this book will address in more detail later. The bottom line is that these writers agree that a person can still be thoroughly Evangelical in his commitment to Jesus Christ and the inerrancy of Scripture and challenge conventional thinking regarding the traditional oppression/possession paradigm often used to explain spiritual warfare.

Scripture allows and experience indicates that typical oppression/possession paradigm divisions are not adequate to fully explain all of our temptations and struggles. Missionaries have discussed the problem of demonic bondage among genuine believers for years. But we are often slow hearing, much less accepting, things that make us feel uncomfortable. If we accept the possibility of a Christian under actual demonic attack, which is more severe than oppression but not the total domination and control commonly referred to as demonic possession, spiritual warfare becomes a more complicated subject than a conventional oppression/possession paradigm model suggests.

Imagine a house standing by itself on a hill lit up brightly against the dark night. It has twenty-seven rooms, and every one of them blazes with light. If you are wandering around lost in the pitch dark night, you would be grateful for the light shining from every single room. The more bright rooms you see in the night the easier your road to safety and the greater your hope—the greater the light, the greater the hope.

Could you see this house from far off if several rooms were dark? Yes—but the fewer rooms there are with light, the more difficult it is find safety. In fact, if most of the lights are out, even though that house contrasts with the pitch darkness around it, you would have trouble spotting and following its light.

The word translated *foothold* or *opportunity* in Ephesians 4:27—*and do not give the devil an opportunity*—had several common meanings in Greek literature that may help contextually in this discussion. According to Bauer, Arndt and Gingrich's *A Greek-English Lexicon Of The New Testament And Other Early*

Christian Literature,[1] the word *topos* can mean: A) inhabited place, B) inhabited space, place, C) place, location, D) regions, districts, E) place, room to live, stay, sit etc., F) the place where something is found, G) the place to which a person's final destiny brings him. In special circumstances the word could also mean: a) a place or passage, b) position or office, and c) possibility, opportunity or chance.

Question. Is it possible for a person who owns a home to rent out rooms or for a person who leases a house to sub-rent rooms without affecting either house's actual ownership? An owner can rent the house to good renters who will help care for the house or to poor renters who will destroy it. But whether he rents to good or bad tenants doesn't change the actual legal owner of that house. He is still the owner even if he is foolish enough to allow a renter to destroy the rooms available to him. The owner has legal authority to have a bad renter removed. But it won't happen if he doesn't exercise his legal authority. Renters can threaten and intimidate the true owner or cry and spin stories of woe to induce guilt. But neither threats nor tears can legally keep the owner from handing a destructive renter a properly notarized eviction notice.

As a Christian, I can choose to walk controlled by the Spirit and yield my whole temple to God, which is my reasonable service. But it is also possible for me to willfully choose to refuse to yield select rooms, or areas of my life, to the control of the Holy Spirit through unconfessed sin. If it is not my desire to submit every room of my house to God then I consciously or unconsciously have hung out a sign to demons reading "Vacancy—Rooms Available."

My choice to rent out rooms in my life is a foolish decision, but it does not change the fact that God is still the legal owner of my life. When I am ready to hand out eviction notices He certainly has the authority to enforce those notices. Christians who choose to give footholds to Satan through unconfessed sin, possibly thinking

---

[1] University of Chicago Press, 1957, pp. 830–831.

it is just a game, are potentially surrendering areas of their lives to demonic control one room at a time. Jesus' lordship over every area of our lives is not just a game. Usually the longer an owner allows a bad renter to destroy rooms the more rooms he will destroy. Failure to confront a problem in our lives is usually an invitation for more problems.

Any light is more than no light and a contrast to darkness. The more rooms I surrender to darkness the less hope I provide to the lost wanderer looking for help. Our job is to shine as lights in the midst of a crooked and perverse generation. Hanging "Vacancy" signs does not further the cause of Christ. In fact, when we allow the rental and darkening of more rooms than we keep swept, cleaned and surrendered to the control of the Holy Spirit, we diminish our house's effectiveness as a source of light.

Is it possible for a demon to possess (totally/completely control and subjugate) a Christian? No. Remember, demons do not own anything, they are squatters. There is only one true owner for a Christian, and that is God who created us and bought us at a very great price. Is it possible for demonic spirits to oppress a Christian? Yes, Christians are the favorite target of demonic archers. We are, after all, their enemies. Scripture does not promise us complete freedom from flaming darts in this life. What Scripture does promise is that our shield of faith will extinguish them. Is it possible for a Christian to experience demonization, invasion or infestation? Yes it is. Demonic spirits can, to varying degrees, control Christians. Scripture allows it, and experience confirms it. Is a demonized Christian still a Christian? Yes again. All Christians have received God's guarantee that we belong to Him, the Holy Spirit who lives inside us, and the promise that He will never leave or forsake us. A true Christian can therefore, never be totally, completely or absolutely controlled or dominated by demons. Non-Christians have no such divine guarantee or promise to stand on or to protect them.

God has given us our earthly bodies on loan. We can foolishly choose to sub-rent rooms of the house God has temporarily loaned us, but the house's ownership is not ours to give away.

A friend said that he would be much more comfortable using a different metaphor regarding a demon's ability to attach to a believer than invading a room of a genuine Christian's house. I suggested that one might see demons as leeches with the ability to attach themselves to believers with the intent of sucking their life blood and testimony for Christ dry. If I decide to swim in a river or pond with leeches, I shouldn't be surprised that I may have to pull leeches off different areas of my body when I get out of the water. Whether a person views demons as entering a room through an open door or as attaching themselves to a person's body, the important thing to realize is that demons seem to have the ability to connect themselves to true Christians. Whether the area they occupy is physical, mental or possibly both, I do not know. I am also not certain when a person crosses the line that allows a demon to take control of an area of their life. These lines differ among believers. But from the inspired language of Ephesians 4:27 it appears that they potentially have the ability to occupy or control rooms or space in or on a true believer. The personal experiences of solidly Evangelical Christians, church leaders and missionaries consistently support this conclusion, too.

Is this demonic possession? No. A demon does not own the believer. But a Christian who has given ground, space or territory to demons is certainly in a condition that is more difficult to deal with than one due to the deceptive darts of simple external oppression.

I know it can trouble some people theologically to think about the possibility of demons having the opportunity to connect themselves to true believers or to gain access or control in areas of the body or mind of a true Christian. A common question, and a fair one at this point, is: *Would God really allow a demon to occupy a room in a home He owns*? (This question used to bother me. It no longer does.) God certainly allows the flesh to continue to actively work against His purposes in the life of a Christian if that person allows it. In fact, 1 Corinthians 2:14–3:3 indicate the possibility for the flesh to so control and dominate a genuine Christian that the person's actions do not appear much different than those of a natural man. According to Galatians 5:16, Christians can choose whether the Spirit or the flesh controls them. However, Galatians 5:17 and Romans 7:15–25 make it clear that our conflict with the flesh is a fact of life and an ongoing daily reality of Christian living, even for sincere and dedicated believers.

Question. If God allows the flesh or old nature, which is at enmity with Him, to remain active in the life of a true Christian, why is it so difficult to understand or believe that demons have the ability to exercise limited control in the lives of Christians who are foolish enough to allow them a space of control, i.e. Ephesians 4:26–27? We believe and teach that God alone is omnipresent. Every other created thing, no matter how intelligent or powerful, is still created and finite. This being the case, there is only one way to consistently argue that God would never share any space with our old nature or a demon: We would have to argue that He is unwilling to indwell the body of a true Christian. Numerous verses in the New Testament, including 1 Corinthians 3:16, 6:19–20, and Ephesians 1:13–14, argue clearly and unequivocally that this is simply not true. Christians are temples of God because He does live within each born-again person. Deists may believe God exists but lives in isolation of His creation, but the Bible does not support that view.

What kind of opportunity did Paul have in mind when he warned his Christian readers that their failure to deal quickly with sin could potentially give Satan or his demons a place, space, location, region, room, position or chance? Is this place or space Satan may have the opportunity to control real or just theoretical? Is this space physical, mental, either one or neither one? As hard as it is for some to accept, if context rather than theological bias determines how we approach a passage, it is not difficult to see that the normal reading of this passage includes the possibility that believers can give up areas of control in their lives to demons.

Aren't demons really more interested in bothering people with high visibility like Billy Graham or Chuck Swindoll than low profile Christians like most of us?

I've always heard that it's not normal Christians but crazy people who foam at the mouth, roll on the floor, talk to people who aren't there, display excessive strength, worship the devil, have supernatural powers or run around naked and cut themselves who struggle with demons. But, on the contrary, my subjective experience has consistently confirmed other Christians' testimony that this type of generalization is simply not true.

Doesn't this kind of reasoning represent the same type of thinking that Christians involved in the abortion and sexual immorality debate oppose? If we hear enough times that abortion is our right and premarital or extramarital sexual involvement of nearly any type is an acceptable lifestyle, then regardless of what the Bible teaches, we are supposed to nod our heads and agree or face the wrath of those whose politically correct agenda we reject. Repetition doesn't make something necessarily true or false. But how many sincere Christians who reject the idea that repetition and convenience rather than the Bible make an argument right in the abortion and sexual morality debates turn around and use repetition and convenience rather than the Bible as the basis for vehemently arguing an oppression/possession only position in this debate?

How do demonic spirits usually attack Christians?

The most common method of attack I have discovered in working with believers struggling under demonic affliction is habitual debilitating and paralyzing mental accusation. Scripture makes it clear that this is consistent with Satan's strategic operation. This also helps explain the nature of the fiery darts Paul warns Christians in Ephesians 6:10–18 to defend against.

Finally, be strong in the Lord, and in the strength of His might. Put on the full armor of God, that you may be able to stand firm against the schemes of the devil. For our struggle is not against flesh and blood, but against the rulers, against the powers,

*against the world forces of this darkness, against
the spiritual forces of wickedness in the heavenly
places. Therefore, take up the full armor of God,
that you may be able to resist in the evil day, and
having done everything, to stand firm...In addition
to all, taking up the shield of faith with which you
will be able to extinguish all the flaming missiles of
the evil one.* Ephesians 6:10–13, 16.

While speaking to a large group of career singles on the
subject of "spiritual warfare," one of the young men challenged
me. He said he didn't think he had ever come under attack by
demonic accusation. I was glad he made the statement and shared
with him and the rest of the group that I bet the real issue was not
the reality of this type of attack, but rather our ability to identify its
true source.

I then shared the same illustration that I have used
numerous times in different parts of the country when dealing with
this topic. I mentioned that although the names and circumstances
would probably be different, the principles are the same.

Spungetta and Floradora are finishing a conversation in the
local supermarket parking lot. As Spungetta is walking toward her
car she hears an all too familiar voice whisper:

*Tell Floradora you are sorry for the cruel remarks
you made about her and confess your sin to God.*

The problem is that Spungetta cannot honestly remember making
any cruel remarks to her best friend. Not wanting to be disobedient
to the conviction she assumes is from the Holy Spirit though, she
decides she had better obey and pray anyway just to be sure she is
covering her spiritual bases.

*God, forgive me for whatever it was I said that was
wrong. I'm sorry about that and will call Floradora
when I get home to get it right with her. Amen.*

After whispering a quick prayer asking for forgiveness for her
apparent sin and promising God she will clear up the issue with
Floradora as soon as possible, she continues her walk to her car.

But before she can reach it, another distinct thought, voice, impression or idea quickly filters through her mind:

> *That prayer was trite and lacked conviction. You didn't begin by saying "Our Father" and didn't end "in Jesus' Name." Pray again and this time with sincerity and feeling.*

Spungetta thinks, *I guess I did pray pretty fast and flippantly. I'd better pray again, only this time with more sincerity, remembering to begin "Dear Father" and closing "in Jesus' Name."* After a second prayer, which she assumes will close the issue and bring the peace that should accompany a clear conscience, she has the distinct thought:

> *Don't you believe God answered your prayer the first time you prayed? Why did you pray a second time about the same issue unless you don't really believe God answers your prayers? Does God care about your words or the attitude of your heart? Confess your lack of faith and the sin of double-mindedness to God.*

Frustrated but obedient, Spungetta asks God to forgive her for her doubt and the lack of faith she demonstrated by praying a second time for something He answered the first time, even though she still isn't sure exactly what her sin was in the first place.

Then, before she can get her keys into the car door to unlock it she hears:

> *You were supposed to share the faith with the two ladies parked next to you. But while you were praying insincerely and demonstrating a lack of faith, those two women who just drove off are headed to a Christless eternity, and their blood is on your hands. How many people are going to hell because of your lack of faith? A real Christian would know that God always answers prayers the first time. Now you've failed a perfect witnessing opportunity, and you still don't think you've done*

> *anything wrong? Tell God how sorry you are for*
> *being such a faithless ambassador and jeopardizing*
> *the eternal salvation of those He loved enough to*
> *die for.*

With feelings of remorse, despair and growing frustration, Spungetta will ask God to forgive her for her failure to use the witnessing opportunities God set up for her because she was busy doubting Him and confessing and re-confessing sins that she felt guilty for but still couldn't specifically identify. Does it usually end here? No. As she gets into her car and turns the ignition on she hears that same quiet voice she assumes is the Holy Spirit say to her:

> *Christian living is supposed to be a joy, but for you*
> *it's always a job. Nothing comes easy for you like it*
> *does your friends. Since God is in control of*
> *everything, why doesn't He help you? It's because*
> *you don't really belong to Him. True Christians*
> *walk in victory, but you are a failure. Other*
> *Christians don't miss divine opportunities to witness*
> *because they are busy doubting God and re-*
> *confessing forgiven sins. Why don't you give up? If*
> *you promise God you will pray more faithfully and*
> *memorize more Scripture, you will probably just*
> *break those promises too, so just do God a favor*
> *and die. You will still go to heaven, but think of all*
> *the people you will no longer confuse by your lack*
> *of faith and inconsistent lifestyle.*

As ridiculous as it sounds sitting outside of this conversation, many Christians live in this type of mental hell every single day. No matter how sincere they are and how hard they try to please God, it just seems like it is never enough. That accusing voice can always quote one more verse or come up with one more reason why you are a failure who will never find peace or a permanent place in God's love.

As I shared that simple scenario that day with those singles I saw the same reaction I have witnessed time and time again. Eyes began to drop, and heads began to nod. Several individuals became visibly red-eyed. Eventually, comments will surface like:

> *So that's what accusation is about. I have lived with*
> *this most of my life but just figured it's the way I*
> *think or a cross I must bear for Christ. I've never*
> *told anybody about this because I already feel*
> *isolated and alone and figure sharing something*
> *like this with someone could isolate me even*
> *further.*

I liken this endless circle of accusation to a hamster running round and round in a cage on his wheel. As a child, I had a hamster. Most of the time I wasn't even conscious of what seemed like his non-stop running on his little circular track. But sometimes the noise of the wheel going round woke me up at night. I felt sorry for the hamster because no matter how slow or fast it ran it always remained in the same spot at the bottom of the wheel. All that energy and time spent for what?

There are hundreds and thousands of Christians on the receiving end of the fiery arrows of demonic accusation who secretly feel very much like that little hamster. No matter how hard they try or how dedicated they are in their Christian lives, they never seem able to progress beyond the bottom of the wheel and the feeling of being trapped inside the cage of their mind and thoughts. The only thing all their efforts seem to produce is mental confusion and emotional exhaustion.

Predictable feelings of failure and frustration are followed by promises to pray longer and study more. Eventually, such individuals will listen to the voices long enough and begin to believe them, deciding that maybe things never will change and possibly they would actually be better off dead.

The wheel of accusation will go full circle when the individual grows weary of blaming himself for repeated failures and decides that if God really loved him he wouldn't be in this mental mess in the first place. Feelings of resentment and bitterness directed at God and other Christians will often replace feelings of discouragement and inadequacy. "It's His fault. It's their fault."

The problem at this point will often produce deep feelings of guilt when the individuals realize they are blaming God who is the only person in the world who truly loves them. This, in turn, intensifies inner feelings of utter failure and uselessness with depression, hopelessness or apathy being the end result.

As the Christian struggles with this guilt and false guilt, the accuser mocks and laughs.

> *Run, you stupid little hamster. You are a failure. Do yourself and God a favor and just die. You don't experience victory in your life. You never have. Your testimony is a lie. You are worthless to yourself, others and God. Do everybody a favor and end all of your pain and suffering. You are a bother to others.*

As Christians, we play into the hand of Satan and his demonic host when we approach warfare as a novel game or curiosity rather than as a life-threatening conspiracy from the pit of hell. While we try to see how "normal" we can still appear to other Christians and our non-Christian colleagues and neighbors, demonic accusers relentlessly plot our destruction. When we approach prayer, Bible study and the assembling of ourselves together as a necessary obligation to fit into our busy schedule rather than the privilege it really is, we find ourselves taking dart after dart, hit after hit, and wondering why God is not protecting us.

What should you do if you were on a warship sailing in the ocean and enemy airplanes were attacking you from above? A good starting point would be to carefully aim and shoot anti-aircraft guns at the enemy planes trying to bomb your ship. If your ship is dodging torpedoes that an enemy submarine is shooting from underwater, would you again aim your aircraft guns skyward and blast away? Not unless you want to have fellowship with Charley the Tuna on the bottom of the ocean.

Anti-aircraft guns are defensive protection for ships against enemy airplanes. Depth charges protect warships from enemy submarines lurking below the water. Who is really at fault if the operators of the defense systems are killing seagulls by the hundreds while a submarine is attacking them or blowing up fish by the thousands while enemy airplanes drop bombs on their decks? Do we blame the designer of the defense systems or the operators who are shooting good ammunition at the wrong objects? Athletes study their playbooks so they can compete at an optimal level. They understand that if they don't know their playbooks, they won't play in the game. Too many Christians see the study of their playbook, the Bible, as an inconvenient obligation to endure and wonder why their Christian lives are so ineffective and boring.

I am afraid that often Satan must look at our actions as Christians as little more than a bad joke rather than those of an enemy of concern because of our delegated authority in Christ Jesus. We are soldiers for the cross of Christ. Our weapons are not fleshly but divinely powerful (2 Corinthians10:3–5). However, God expects us to know enough about the weapons systems He has designed for our protection that we can correctly match the right system with the right enemy.

As cliché-ish as it may sound, our Bible is our operator's manual. When our attitude is that we are doing God a favor by reading it once in a while, it's not hard to guess who is going to lose most of the battles. Victory for Christians involved in spiritual warfare begins with being able to identify our enemies and correctly respond to their various schemes. To do less is to look as silly as people on a ship shooting seagulls while the enemy is blowing large holes in it below the waterline. As believers with authority delegated from the Lord Jesus Christ, victory is ultimately ours over all the power of the enemy. But we can and will continue to lose battles to a highly organized and evil army until we learn to train and fight Biblically rather than to sit around, apathetically lamenting the fact that too many of the battles go to the other side.

How do demons typically take advantage of Christians?

Demons have two primary avenues for controlling Christians. Ephesians 4:25–27 explains the first and most common.

Therefore, laying aside falsehood, SPEAK TRUTH, EACH ONE of you, WITH HIS NEIGHBOR, for we are members of one another. Be ANGRY, AND yet DO NOT SIN; do not let the sun go down on your anger, and do not give the devil an opportunity.

The word "opportunity" means a handhold or foothold. When we fail to keep short accounts with sin we provide footholds or handholds that allow Satan to take advantage of us. To think he will not exploit these holds is naive. If Satan was bold enough to confront the Son of God, who among men could possibly think he would not dare approach them? Remember, a demon's purpose is to destroy, not just annoy.

Think of a person trying to climb a slick mountain that goes straight up. This would be a very difficult challenge for even an experienced mountain climber, but it wouldn't be impossible. If I have a piton hammer and enough time, I can chip out a handhold. If I have more time, I can switch hands with the hammer and keep chipping. Give me enough time, and I can carve out niches not only for my hands but my feet, too. Slowly but surely I will climb up a smooth straight surface.

If I choose to concentrate my efforts on a particular spot, I can turn a niche for my fingers into a hole large enough to stick in my fist. The more time I have to chip away, the more secure my position will become. When I fail to deal with my sin, I provide Satan, or more likely his helpers, the opportunity to start chipping out hand and footholds in my life. What starts as a fingertip grip will end up a firm handhold attempting to control and strangle me. I can stop the process when I choose to confess my sin rather than ignore it. But as long as I choose to play the game, I am going to pay the dues. And the longer the games go on, the more severe the consequences will become.

How does a godly person find himself in a compromising position? Compromise usually begins with baby steps. I do not believe Christian leaders blatantly jump into sexually compromising relationships. They start by flirting with fire and crossing lines they know they should avoid rather than entertain. This downward spiral of mental rationalization will usually progress from a light guiding influence to a controlling death grip over a period of time. The process works the same way for all of us. The results of compromise are just more visible and damaging when it involves leaders. The privilege of leading carries a corresponding responsibility that can produce great blessing or promote destructive bitterness depending upon whether the person uses or abuses that privilege.

In principle, there is no difference between the process that puts compromised leaders in this position and the life of the individual who quietly and secretly lives in sin. Both assume that they can fool Satan and God as long as they can fool people. Satan is harder to cheat than men and women. But no one can cheat God. We can choose whether or not to play the games, but we are seldom able to control the consequences of our sin.

The good news is that when we keep short accounts with God regarding our sin, Satan doesn't have the time or opportunity to chip holes in our lives or body armor. And if he already has, it is possible to confess the sin(s) that allowed the problem(s) and to ask God to fill in the hole(s) and smooth the surface so there is once again no way for an enemy to gain a secure hand or foothold against us.

The second entry point for demons into the life of a Christian involves ancestral sin. Whether it seems fair or not, demons can take advantage of Christians through the sins of their ancestors. Ancestral sin is not as typical as the slow erosion of unconfessed sin, but it is still a real possibility that I am seeing on an increasing basis.

I believe the reason I am seeing more of this than even ten years ago is because as sin becomes more and more fashionable and godly living becomes less and less politically correct, people are making themselves and their children easier targets. Children can receive a blessing from growing up in a godly home. They also can suffer extreme consequences for the games parents play when they assume no one is looking or keeping account. The implications of the destructive consequences of ancestral sin as they relate directly or indirectly to children born into a culture and generation that openly rejects the existence of moral absolutes, regards evangelical Christianity a destructive opiate, and embraces and absolutizes postmodernism, relativism and tolerance as the new golden rule is staggering in its potential destruction.

God repeats the same basic message regarding ancestral sin in Exodus 20:4–5, 34: 6–7, Numbers 14:18, Deuteronomy 5: 9–10 and Jeremiah 32:18 that the New Testament nowhere abrogates.

> *The LORD, the LORD God, compassionate and gracious, slow to anger, and abounding in loving kindness and truth; who keeps loving kindness for thousands, who forgives iniquity, transgression and sin; yet He will by no means leave the guilty unpunished, visiting the iniquity of fathers on the children and on the grandchildren to the third and fourth generations.* Exodus 34:6b–7

How important is the will of a demonized person seeking freedom through Christ?

Usually the first meeting I have with an individual interested in exploring the possibility of demonization is to determine, to the best of my ability, if he is truly a Christian and to discuss the importance of his will. The person's relationship with Christ and his will to walk with Him are more important than my participation. I am just a Christian brother who has been through this battle with hundreds of others before him. We share the same authority and position in Christ. I can encourage the individual to stand in Christ and fight, but I cannot stand or fight for him.

Is the person here because he is ready to volitionally submit his entire life to the lordship of Christ, or is he here because someone made him seek help against his will? Has a person decided to deal with this issue because she is repentant of her sin or is she just annoyed with the consequences and price tag that accompany poor choices?

> *I want help but I don't want to change my lifestyle*
> *or priorities. I'm upset I got caught in my sin, but*
> *I'm not really sorry it happened. I want help getting*
> *rid of the consequences of my sin, but I will make*
> *sure I don't get caught in the future.*

Unconfessed sin gives demonic spirits a foothold or ground against a believer. Holding ground is a phrase used by demons to explain their ability to exercise limited control over a place, space, territory or specific area of a Christian's life. Once a person is willing to confess his sins and ask God to cancel the ground held against him, the battle is relatively simple. The believer has in effect given an eviction notice to an unwanted renter or swatted a bloodsucking leech. God, who is omnipotent, has no problem enforcing the eviction notice for an individual who submits to Him with clean hands and a pure heart.

But what about the person playing games? My consistent experience is that demons will not voluntarily leave individuals who are unwilling to fully submit every area of their lives to God. I have spent many frustrating hours working with double-minded or weak-willed Christians who want relief from demonic bondage but who are unwilling to deal honestly with the issues that opened the doors in the first place. It is as though they want to say "No" to Satan, but they are still unwilling to say "Yes" to God. Straddling the line may work well for politicians more concerned with re-election than with doing what is right, but it is not possible to straddle the line of obedience to God with demons. If a person is not actively resisting demonic activity, he is both inviting it and ultimately allowing it to continue.

I will no longer agree to assist Christians who are running from God. We will both just end up frustrated. I usually ask them to come back when or if they are looking up from the bottom and have decided to fight like victorious soldiers for Christ rather than to sit like victimized spectators. Passivity, fear, bitterness and indifference to sin each represent an invitation for demonization.

During our first meeting I typically give an individual a lesson and assignment on substitutive thinking. Win in your head and you will win in your life. Lose in your head, and it is only a matter of time before you will be losing in life.

Two books have been extremely helpful for me in explaining the concepts of renewing our minds and substitutive thinking. The first is *Counter Attack* by Jay Carty (Yes Ministries). The second is *Getting to No: How to Break a Stubborn Habit* by Erwin Lutzer (Moody Press).

When my car grinds to a stop I do not immediately call a tow truck to haul it to a service center and have the engine or transmission torn apart. The first thing I check is my gas gauge. Next, I open the hood and check my belts, battery cables and spark plug wires. If the simple things don't work, then I allow someone to dig deeper. It's embarrassing and expensive to call in a professional repairman and find out that the problem was common sense rather than technical.

If a person consistently practices renewing his mind and the "problem" goes away, there is no reason to blame demons. If, on the other hand, individuals discipline themselves to right thinking, and the debilitating accusations and fears do not stop, I will encourage them to come back. At that point they are usually much more willing to seriously address the possibility of demonic warfare. For most people confronting demons is a last resort. Right thinking will not remove demons. It will anger and frustrate them, but they will not leave unless the person first confesses the sin and cancels the ground. Scripture memorization and right thinking are necessary priorities for Christian living, but they are not sufficient in and of themselves to remove demons if that person already has given ground. As Christians we have delegated authority and power to confront and remove demonic strongholds, but we must learn to address spiritual warfare Biblically rather than just sincerely.

Christians who consistently win more battles with demons than they lose have learned how to both recognize and respond to demonic archers. Although running is one Biblical response for a

Christian confronting the flesh, it is never a Biblical response for confronting demons. The Bible commands Christians to *resist* demonic opposition, not run from it (James 4:7–10; 1 Peter 5:6–9). Guesswork does not produce effective results at school or in warfare!

7

Demonic Warfare:
Blatant or Stealth?

D emonic warfare is usually a battle of mental subtleties and deception that more often than not focuses upon growing Christians. If you think about it for a moment this makes sense. Propositions to boldly and blatantly jump into obvious sin will not easily fool most Christians who are sincere in their faith, obedient in service and wanting to mature spiritually in their relationship with God on a daily basis. If demonic archers want to slow down a dedicated Christian, they must do more than simply promote the predictable.

Ironically, but logically, there seems a direct correlation between a believer's devotion and commitment level and the subtle attention and attacks demonic spirits direct towards that person. The bottom line seems that the more dedicated and consistent a Christian is, the more that person must face the enemy's fiery arrows. It's common sense. A good military general is going to align his best troops against his strongest opposition. Why should he commit a large number of forces to oppose an impotent enemy who poses no direct threat?

The Christian controlled by fear might conclude that the less consistently he follows Jesus, the fewer demonic attacks he will have to endure. Once again, the logic works, but the motivation is disgraceful. Ultimately, fear motivates this type of thinking, and fear is a terrible motivator for a person who understands that if God is for you, it doesn't really matter who is against you (Romans 8:31). Why should a Christian believe a lie that implies Satan has more power to attack than God has power to protect?

> *Don't get involved in spiritual warfare. If you do, they will get you.*

Don't buy the lie. Even if this type of comment is popular and spoken sincerely, fear is still its motivation. We must remember when discussing spiritual warfare that we are on the side that has ultimately won the war, not the side that lost. One result of victory in Christ Jesus over Satan and his demons is that Christians should live life as victors, not victims (Romans 8). Our position right now is that we are seated in heaven with Jesus, far above all rule and authority (Ephesians 2:6). Our master, Jesus, has already defeated Satan (Ephesians 1:18–23, Colossians 2:15, 1 John 3:8). As long as we are identified with Jesus, we do not have to fear a defeated enemy (Luke 10:18–20, Hebrews 2:14, 1 Peter 5:6–9).

Demonic activity in North America

In this chapter I will address several issues related to subtleties of spiritual warfare and the Christian. Why would demonic activity in North America *appear* so restrained today in contrast to the stories in the Bible and reports we often hear from missionaries in developing or Third World countries? One would assume that if demons are organized and systematic in their operations that their methods would appear essentially the same regardless of whom, when or where they attack.

Doesn't the fear of demonism simply represent the pathetic and naive superstitious phobias of a more primitive time in man's physical, spiritual, philosophical and mental evolution? As mentioned earlier, it should be no surprise that the more sophisticated a person or society assumes itself, the more subtle and crafty its enemies' subterfuges must become to be effective. Demons attempt to destroy their enemies. They do not play at their work or take vacations. They work in deadly earnest. Demons approach their assigned responsibilities from a win/lose mentality. They fight to win and work diligently to make Christians lose. They clearly understand what Jesus meant when He declared that a house divided against itself will fall. Demons play to win, and they play for keeps with every calculated move they make.

This certainly puts them at a distinct advantage over many Christians who seem comfortable dismissing or ridiculing their existence and the reality of spiritual warfare. In so doing, such Christians relegate a believer's conflict with demons to childish ghost stories or to discomforting phenomena missionaries overseas might occasionally confront but that "ordinary" Christians can simply ignore.

Why does demonic warfare in industrialized nations seem less demonstrative than in developing countries? The bottom line is that subtle covert attacks in our society are usually more effective than aggressive overt attacks that could possibly wake up even the most religious skeptics to question the reality, relevance and correctness of spiritual faith, doctrinal presuppositions and theistic worldviews.

If you were a demon and you received orders to destroy a person living in a culture steeped in animism and fear, would you approach that person the same way you would a biochemist trained at Harvard and living in Boston? Attempting to convince a person who has spent the majority of his life trying to appease evil spirits that supernatural entities do not exist is probably not an effective plan of attack. But terrorizing this same person through open attacks and bizarre manifestations and communicating a message that his gods are not strong enough to protect him from the wrath of an offended demon might effectively allow the demon to continue manipulating and controlling him.

On the other hand, ridiculing both Christianity and demonism as emotional hocus pocus and the sign of a weak, gullible mind could be a very effective way to keep a proud, self-made, rationalist and empiricist, impressed with his own education, opinions and accomplishments, from even exploring the possibilities of spirituality in general, demonic warfare specifically or the gospel message of new life in Jesus Christ. The cost of honest exploration might seem too great a price to pay among skeptical colleagues. Satan and his demons are masters of creating confusion and deception, and understand that to be effective it is necessary to fight smarter, not just harder.

People who are critical of Christians, Jesus, the Bible, Christianity and miracles are essentially looking for reasons to reaffirm their belief that religion is just the opiate of the naive, and a mental crutch for weak-willed people who are looking for someone else to think for them. Overt activity that challenges their basic anti-supernatural worldview could, therefore, become counter-productive. Why wake up people who are spiritually asleep, haplessly bobbing on the waves of naturalism and happily adrift in a sea of moral, ethical and religious relativism? If someone or something made the mistake of arousing them from their stupor, they might actually become motivated to take some type of aggressive action. A more effective plan is to let them stay drugged in their hubris and religious skepticism, sound asleep and devoid of any understanding of spiritual realities.

People typically view demonic activity as outside the normal Christian experience. They may ignore it as the boorish hysteria of primitive people, study it as the pitiful excesses of mentally imbalanced religious fanatics fixated upon demons or embrace it as a desirable authenticating spiritual experience of enlightened New Age devotees.

We live in a society often led by people who think they are too sophisticated academically and advanced technologically to consider the subject of the supernatural. Thus, it makes sense that demons would choose to lie low rather than to openly manifest themselves in a culture content to worship the creation rather than the Creator.

Subtle and harmless are often a more effective strategy for controlling and manipulating than direct and confrontational. For instance, how many growing Christian women would allow a handsome man who said the following to make them awestruck?

Hey baby, I've been looking at your body and imagining what you look like undressed. You are a fine piece of meat, and I want to use you for my lustful enjoyment tonight. I made a bet with a friend that I could take home any woman in this room, and you're the lucky object of my charm and deception. Let's have a party for two all night long. I've got a bottle chilled and smooth jazz waiting just for you tonight at my cozy crib. Think too long and you're going to miss out on me and the night of your life.

A growing Christian would probably smack him or laugh in his face, but she certainly wouldn't respond with anything other than the contempt that this type of self-serving narcissistic moron deserves. But what would happen if that same handsome hunk approached that same Christian woman and said:

I recently lost my best friend to cancer. He was a good person and God let him die. I can't understand why? My parents divorced when I was young, and relatives passed me from house to house for years. I was never wanted. As a result I've never done very well in school because I was never encouraged to study. I was always busy taking care of my nieces and nephews. I figured since I was imposing upon my relatives by living with them, the least I could do was take care of their children. Whenever I went to their church I always felt funny because I knew their friends were aware that I was an outsider they were stuck with because of family obligation. I felt so alone. All I have ever wanted was a family. It made me feel like crying out, "Why me, God?

I need your help learning how to get to know God. I need help learning how to forgive, but you probably don't have time. I'm sure it will only be a matter of time before someone tells you not to associate with someone like me. But I believe God sent you to me as an angel of mercy and that you're different. You're kind, and your faith in God is real. I believe you can help me become the real person God wants me to become. Didn't Jesus associate with tax collectors? He helped people in need even if He had to get His hands a little dirty. You're kind and forgiving. I can tell you love people and you don't judge others. I think you're a beautiful person inside and outside. Would you be willing to meet with me for Bible study and prayer so I can learn how to be the kind of person God wants me to be? I really need your help.

There are men who are more than willing to feed a "nice Christian" woman's maternal, protective, caring desire to fix hurts, if that's what it takes to get past her defenses. In a context of dating relationships I often refer to this type of deception and manipulation as the *Scraggly Kitty Syndrome*. Here's how it works. Scraggly Kitties are masters at manipulating a person's feelings and emotions. To a Scraggly Kitty, women represent nothing more than a convenient challenge, a free lunch, a warm bed and someone to sexually and financially use and abuse until it's time to move on once again.

The people who know his antics and remain unimpressed by his silver tongue and stories of woe put the Scraggly Kitty out. But he is smart, and he is a survivor. He complains about how unfair life is and all the bad breaks he's received. Guys tell him to quit whining, and savvy women tell him to take a walk. But there are other women who are long on feeling emotional pain but short on common sense who will pick up the Scraggly Kitty and say:

Oh Kitty, no one understands you like I do. Everyone has been so mean to you. I will give you a bath, comb out your tangles, feed you and let you sleep by my warm fire. I won't let anyone hurt you ever again.

The Scraggly Kitty will purr, snuggle up and tell this woman that she's different but that sooner or later she'll abandon him just like all the rest. This, of course, leads her to promise that she'll never let that happen, which puts a wry smile on the face of Kitty. After the Scraggly Kitty begins to warm up and become more comfortable, he will act like the mangy manipulator he really is. He will display the type of character that has destroyed previous friendships and relationships. By the time the Christian woman finally sees why others have put this loser out and that it's time to do the same, the Scraggly Kitty will remind his tenderhearted meal ticket of her promises never to abandon him like everyone else did.

> *I thought you were different. I thought Christians kept their word. I was wrong, and you're just like all the rest. I'll never go to church or read the Bible again, and it's your fault. I guess I just can't trust anyone, not even God.*

Scraggly Kitties give Good Samaritans a bad name. Unfortunately, a sister who will fall for the Scraggly Kitty in the first place is also the same person who will allow guilt to manipulate her and say:

> *Oh no. I'm sorry. What was I thinking about? I promised that I'd be true to you even when others are not. I try to be a woman of God. I made a promise to care for you, and I'll keep my promise as unto God, even if it is to my own hurt.*

Do you remember Scar in the movie *Lion King*? Scar was a perfect depiction of a manipulative Scraggly Kitty who was willing to use pity, guilt, trust and the betrayal of innocence to get his own way, even if it meant using his enemies or killing his own family members to accomplish his evil plans.

I should mention one final thought regarding scraggly kitties. Do not make the mistake of assuming that this type of manipulation is limited to just deceptive men. There are plenty of women who have learned how to stoke the ego of a gullible Christian man so they can get what they want, one way or another.

More spiritual battles are lost because of deception and mental fatigue fueled by feelings of loneliness and discouragement than by physical affliction. Once soldiers begin questioning what they're fighting for or doubting the adequacy of available resources for winning a battle, they are easier to defeat than when they know who they are, why they are fighting and that they are adequately equipped for any challenge.

Demonic spirits would much rather lull Christians to sleep than risk waking them up. Dopey, mopey believers don't present much of an obstacle to an organized army intent on destroying its enemies. Demons understand that sleepy Christians living an ineffective spiritual life will eventually succumb to apathy. They also understand that typically such Christians have a marginalized testimony motivated by convenience and comfort rather than by courage and conviction.

> *What's the use of living for Christ anyway? Nothing ever changes. Why should I try when I feel like a failure most of the time and nobody seems to care about my testimony for Christ? I know I'm going to heaven, but if I get too fanatical about my faith people could label me as imbalanced, bigoted or a fundamentalist. Those who swim against the flow seldom get raises and promotions. Moderation in all things usually works best in this world, and that probably includes religion too. If I don't rock the boat maybe I won't have to worry about getting tossed out.*

Visible manifestations and direct confrontations with demonic spirits just might serve as a wake-up call for believers stuck in the rut and routine of convenience, compromise, and comfort of playing church. Demons don't want to have to contend with Christians motivated to stand up and fight. They would rather sing "Rock-a-Bye Baby" to snoozing "spiritual warriors" who enjoy singing about victory in Jesus but who refuse to train for spiritual war. They hope to hit, hide and then blame their actions on circumstances or superstitions. Like guerilla fighters, demons want to distract, destroy and annoy right under their enemies' noses. If no one can see them, maybe people will think their work is due to fear, coincidence, paranoia, phobias, mental illness, personality quirks or emotional instability. Fear of the social or theological stigma of association with *the devil made me do it* crowd has effectively ridiculed and silenced many Christian voices on this particular subject for a long time.

Why would a smart demonic spirit risk forcing a confrontation when so many Christians are looking for a reason to avoid the issue of demonization? Emotionalism, stress, an overactive imagination and extremism are easier explanations for demonic activity than being forced to respond to a direct confrontation with demons that visibly manifest themselves.

In the next chapter we will walk step by step through a deliverance process from start to finish. The material is simple, and, pragmatically speaking, it works. Remember, a can of gas is less expensive than work on the engine. But when the problems are demonic, we should praise God that victory and freedom in Christ are possible. It doesn't matter how much ground a person has given up as long as he is willing to yield his whole life to Christ's lordship. Freedom in Christ is a choice—and so is demonic bondage.

8

Demonic Warfare:

How Confrontation Works

In spring 1997, I spoke on the subject of spiritual warfare at a large conference in West Palm Beach, Florida. After the seminar a couple approached who had patiently waited while I was responding to questions. The man was somber, and the woman was sobbing. She told me that she was living in a mental hell and that my examples of demonic accusation with Spongetta and Floradora were her experience every single day. She said she had told her husband that this particular conference was the last one she was going to attend, and it would be her last attempt to get help. She said she had played the part of the devoted and fulfilled minister's wife for years, but that she was tired, angry, bitter and intending to walk away from her husband and family if she didn't get help this weekend. She looked me straight in the eyes and said, "You are it. This seminar is my last try."

Gloria's past sounded like something from a trashy romance novel. Abuse, promiscuity, fear, bitterness, unforgiveness, revenge, voices telling her to give up and kill herself—it was all there. The guilt and constant feelings of unworthiness and failure haunted her on a daily basis in spite of her prayers, Bible reading and tears. After all, as a pastor's wife she was supposed to help other people with their problems, not give up because of her own struggles.

Normally I wouldn't have agreed to work with her without first giving her some homework and reading assignments. Under the circumstances, however, it was clear that if her problems were really a result of demonic attack rather than a lack of faith or spiritual discipline it was necessary to address the issue sooner than later. We found a semi-private room, laid down ground rules and confronted the demonic spirits that had controlling handholds in her life.

The demons had worked very hard, and effectively, too. They had convinced Gloria that she was all alone, unappreciated and a spiritual casualty with no hope of things ever changing, as well as an embarrassment to God, her husband, family and Christian ministry. But she turned into a spiritual tiger when the real source of her anger, guilt and constant feelings of failure and insecurity became apparent. She stood confidently on God's Word and her position in Christ, refusing to allow fear, failure and anger to drive her any longer.

Although this confrontation occurred many years ago, Gloria has remained free of the daily mental and emotional torture and constant demeaning and debilitating accusations that had controlled her thinking most of her adult life. Her husband called me several weeks after we confronted the demons that were attacking and controlling his wife, asking me for more information on Christian demonization. The change in his wife was so dramatic that he was interested in learning how to help other Christians who, like his wife, had not found freedom through more conventional counseling. You see, Gloria had counseled with several fine Christians who addressed her problems as struggles with the world and the flesh. She had even interacted with someone who said he was aware of spiritual opposition. But she had never actually learned how to confront issues rooted in a supernatural source rather than a natural one.

What is the process for removing demons from a demonized person? Is this process transferable so that it is possible to train others, including the demonized individual, to help himself or others caught in this type of bondage? Does this process depend upon a particular type of spiritual giftedness?

These are good questions. Let's begin with the shortest answers first.

Assisting others caught in demonic bondage does not depend upon a particular type of giftedness. Some gifts probably make this type of counseling easier for some than for others. But the authority, victory, protection and position necessary for successfully challenging demons is something freely given to every Christian.

Demons do not typically leave because of the faith or authority of the individual assisting the demonized person. Demons leave because the demonized individual is willing to: 1) confess the sin(s) that provided the foothold in the first place, 2) ask God to cancel the ground or permission given over to the demons, effectively removing their right to stay, and 3) command the controlling demons to leave, standing on the authority, victory, protection and position God purchased and delegated to every true Christian through the cross, resurrection and intercession of the Lord Jesus Christ.

Yes, the process is transferable. A pastor has far too many other responsibilities to be the only individual trained to work with this area of ministry. Ministry is like a pie with many pieces. As a pastor, I need to be available and competent to wear a variety of ministry hats. Evangelism, Bible study, teaching, preaching, pastoral care, counseling, discipleship training, prayer, writing, administrative responsibilities and so forth are all part of a pastor's job description.

If one ministry responsibility totally dominates a leader's schedule, he will neglect other areas unless he is fortunate enough to be one of the privileged few with a large enough staff to cover all the ministry bases so that he has time to specialize. Effective ministry is not one dimensional. Working with demonized

Christians represents one more ministry responsibility effective leaders must learn to recognize and confront.

Christian pastors, counselors and lay leaders have told me they are glad I am comfortable working with this type of problem because they are not. (I count it a privilege to be available to be of help when and where it is possible.) But I am concerned that too often this type of statement is motivated by fear. I've never hung a shingle on my door that says "Exorcist," and I don't intend to in the future. My authority is no different than that of any other Christian. Vocational and lay Christian leaders need to learn how to work with this issue like any other responsibility. To allow our fear or pride to keep those entrusted in our care stuck in bondage is irresponsible. First sermons, funerals, marriages and hospital visitations are usually uncomfortable, too. But they haven't kept effective leaders from learning how to care for these responsibilities.

For many years I've addressed pastors, professional counselors and lay leaders concerning the need for more Christian leaders to become familiar and comfortable working with this area of ministry. It represents one more area of discipleship training. If I can do it, you can, too. I have great respect for Christian counselors trained to help people struggling with physiological, psychological, mental and emotional problems. My respect and admiration runs even higher for those I have now met who incorporate spiritual warfare counseling as part of their practice even though they run the risk of other counselors attacking them for it.

I have referred people to vocational counselors when I was over my head in counseling sessions. I've found though that Christian counselors trained to work with demonic spiritual problems are few and far between. These problems are just as real as mental and physiological problems. Counselors willing to refer clients to someone trained in warfare counseling when they are in over their heads are even harder to find. Isn't it time to admit that we all have more to learn and that referrals can move both directions if our ultimate motive is to help the hurting people entrusted to our care?

A Transferable Process for Confronting Demons

1   A list of problem areas. The first thing I ask people to do if I am going to work with them is to make a list. Using Galatians 5:19–21, Mark 7:21–23 and Colossians 3:5–8 as a basis to launch out, I ask each individual to write down any areas mentioned in these three passages that are habitual problems. These passages describe areas of our battle with the flesh common to man.

> *Now the deeds of the flesh are evident, which are: immorality, impurity, sensuality, idolatry, sorcery, enmities, strife, jealousy, outbursts of anger, disputes, dissensions, factions, envying, drunkenness, carousing, and things like these, of which I forewarn you, just as I have forewarned you, that those who practice such things will not inherit the kingdom of God. (Galatians 5:19–21)*

> *Therefore consider the members of your earthly body as dead to immorality, impurity, passion, evil desire, and greed, which amounts to idolatry. For it is because of these things that the wrath of God will come upon the sons of disobedience, and in them you also once walked, when you were living in them. But now you also, put them all aside: anger, wrath, malice, slander, and abusive speech from your mouth. (Colossians 3:5–8)*

> *"For from within, out of the heart of men, proceed the evil thoughts, fornications, thefts, murders, adulteries, deeds of coveting and wickedness, as well as deceit, sensuality, envy, slander, pride and foolishness. All these evil things proceed from within and defile the man." (Mark 7:21–23)*

If demonization often begins because of unconfessed sin, it makes sense that we should first check those areas identified in the

Bible as common areas of fleshly struggle. I also ask each person to list any other persistent problem areas not listed in any of the passages. For instance, none of those passages mention fear, suicidal depression, eating disorders and constant self-depreciating thoughts. But each of these areas can become a foothold for demonic control.

If the area is not habitual, I ask the person not to write it down. Demons are active, they are unrelenting, and they do their work well. If they are present, they are persistently trying to destroy that person. They will not surface once every decade as a simple annoyance. They like to hide, but they are aggressive in their attempts to control the thinking of the one they hold ground against. Like military beachheads or cancer, they strive to expand their work and the areas they hope to subjugate and conquer.

When a person tells me he got mad because someone carelessly slammed his fingers in the car door, I tell him I would get mad, too. If he says he felt depressed and discouraged because he failed a test or lost a job, I again assure him this also is normal. Areas controlled by demons usually are a constant battleground.

2   **Honesty.** Review with care and clarity the individual's need for complete honesty when confessing sins and asking God to cancel the ground demons hold as a result of those sins. If he holds back or hides areas of sin, the demons will not cooperate, nor do they seem to have to. Even if the person doesn't verbalize it, he is communicating "God can control that area of my life, but not this one." From the demon's perspective, a person who picks and chooses the areas he is willing to submit to God's control is also a person who chooses the areas he is potentially willing to submit to demonic control. If a person does not actively resist demons, then he is willingly entertaining them. This provides an open door for their activity.

3   **Ground rules.** Lay down ground rules for the demons to obey during the entire process.

When I first began working with demonized individuals, I didn't understand the concept of ground rules. I had people yell, scream, swear, cross their eyes, gasp for air, run from my office, fall on the floor in twisted contortions, mock me and those praying and other things I suppose I've probably forgotten over the years.

One afternoon the retired career missionary who helped train me in spiritual warfare counseling asked why I allowed this demonic distraction to happen. I told him that I wasn't aware it could be eliminated. When he asked what ground rules I laid down before confronting the demons, I said I wasn't sure what I could or couldn't do regarding ground rules. He told me that I was subjecting the demonized counselee to far more fear and frustration than necessary by failing to lay down non-negotiable ground rules. Demons, he said, are not equals, and we should not treat them as such. Jesus indicates in Luke 10:18 that Christians have received the authority to step on demons. Laying down ground rules is one way to communicate to demons that they are not in control any longer. My pastor friend gave me a much needed education concerning ground rules that day, and as a result I do not have Christians running out of my office in panic or falling on the floor, cross-eyed and contorted.

The vast majority of the time our office staff doesn't even know whether a particular counseling session I am involved in deals with demonism or people wanting to talk about Bible study, discipleship, marriage, their children or the kingdom of the cults. If warfare counseling is consistently a circus it's because the individual conducting the session either doesn't know what he is doing or he is allowing the chaos on purpose, possibly in an attempt to make himself look more important to the situation than he really is. He creates a problem so he can appear powerful when resolving the very problem he's allowed. From my perspective this is not only an example of immaturity, it's dishonest. Christian leaders are supposed to help people with their problems, not use those problems to promote their own ministries.

If the demonized person has questions about the ground rules there is no problem taking a few minutes to explain each one. More important than understanding each specific rule though is the fact that if there are demons involved, they will understand that our delegated authority is greater than theirs. They will abide by the ground rules whether they like it or not. Demons understand authority. And they know that a Christian's delegated authority is greater than their delegated authority from Satan. They don't like admitting this, but they will acknowledge it when commanded to do so.

The basic purpose of the ground rules is to draw a tight box around the demons. Demons are tricky and desire power, even when we are in the process of commanding them to leave. The ground rules make it clear that they are on the side that has lost, and the counselee is on the side of Christ who has already won. In my opinion, the less we allow demons to speak the better.

What are the ground rules?

The statement, *"In the name of the Lord Jesus Christ"* precedes all the ground rules. The Lord Jesus Christ is our authority, not a rabbit's foot. The purpose of repeating His name is to make it clear to the demons involved that we understand the Lord Jesus Christ is the reason the Christian will win this conflict.

A   *In the name of the Lord Jesus Christ, we bind the strong man. He will not be allowed to interfere in this process in any way. There will be no outside reinforcement of any kind. If there are demons involved with_____, you are on trial and you are going to lose.*

B   *In the name of the Lord Jesus Christ, there will be one-way traffic only, from_____ to the pit. When you leave you will take all of your works and effects and all of your associates and their works and effects with you. You will not be free to re-enter_____ or to enter anyone else in the room.*

C   *In the name of the Lord Jesus Christ, you may speak only that which can be used against you.*

D   *In the name of the Lord Jesus Christ, the answers you give must stand as truth before the white throne of God.*

E   *In the name of the Lord Jesus Christ, there will be no profanity.*

F   *In the name of the Lord Jesus Christ_____is to have complete and full control of his tongue, mind and body. You will not be allowed to control his tongue, mind or body.*

G   *In the name of the Lord Jesus Christ, I will give commands stating "We command" because this is _____'s fight. The Holy Spirit of God is going before us, and we stand as a majority, and we stand together against you. _____ does not want anything to do with you. _____ is a child of God who stands against you. You are an unwanted intruder who is going to have to leave upon command.*

H   *In the name of the Lord Jesus Christ, when I give commands you will give clear, concise, complete answers in _____'s mind to the questions addressed to you. You will not be permitted to confuse the mind of _____ and will be punished severely by the Holy Spirit of God if you attempt to do so.*

I   *When I give commands in the name of the Lord Jesus Christ you will clearly give your answers to _____. You do not have the privilege of speaking directly through him in this confrontation.*

J   *In the name of the Lord Jesus Christ, there will be no hiding, duplicating, or changing of authority and rank. We bind you by the authority structure you now have, and that structure will only be altered if we choose to change it.*

K   *In the name of the Lord Jesus Christ, when I give commands for you to answer, you will give your answers to_____, who will share your responses with me. I will not speak directly to you; you are a defeated enemy not a colleague or an equal, and you are not worth speaking to. I will speak to my brother/sister in Christ. The only thing you are going to do is cooperate under the ground rules. Your authority is smashed!*

L   *Lastly, In the name of the Lord Jesus Christ, we ask the Holy Spirit of God to enforce all of the ground rules and to punish severely any demons who attempt to step outside of the ground rule box.*

Make four declarations that will stand as truth before the white throne of God.

1   We declare our **victory** over all the powers of darkness through our head, the Lord Jesus Christ. We declare that the Lord Jesus Christ has smashed the authority of Satan at the cross of Calvary where He made an open spectacle of your master. Colossians 2:13–15 states:

And when you were dead in your transgressions and the uncircumcision of your flesh, He made you alive together with Him, having forgiven us all our transgressions, having canceled out the certificate of debt consisting of decrees against us and which was hostile to us; and He has taken it out of the way, having nailed it to the cross. When He had disarmed the rulers and authorities, He made a public display of them, having triumphed over them through Him

2   We declare our **authority** over the powers of darkness through the Lord Jesus Christ. In Luke 10:18–20 Jesus told those who follow Him:

And He said to them, I was watching Satan fall from heaven like lightning. Behold I have given you authority to tread upon serpents and scorpions, and over all the power of the enemy, and nothing shall injure you. Nevertheless do not rejoice in this, that the spirits are subject to you, but rejoice that your names are recorded in heaven.

We are aware that our joy is in the fact that our names are recorded in heaven. But we also understand that Jesus Christ has delegated authority to us over all the power of the enemy, subjecting the spirits to us through Him.

3   From the same Luke 10 passage we declare our **protection** from the powers of darkness through our head, the Lord Jesus Christ. Jesus said, "*and nothing shall injure you.*" We declare this to be true through our Lord Jesus Christ and stand upon it.

4   We declare our **position** over the powers of darkness in Jesus Christ. Jesus Christ is our head and we make up His body. Ephesians 1:18–23 says:

I pray that the eyes of your heart may be enlightened, so that you may know what is the hope of His calling, what are the riches of the glory of His inheritance in the saints, and what is the surpassing greatness of His power toward us who believe. These are in accordance with the working of the strength of His might which He brought about in Christ, when He raised Him from the dead, and seated Him at His right hand in the heavenly places, far above all rule and authority and power and dominion, and every name that is named, not only in this age, but also in the one to come. And He put all things in subjection under His feet, and gave Him as head over all things to the church which is His body, the fullness of Him who fills all in all.

Jesus Christ is over all authority, and He is our head. God has put all authority in this age and the one to come under His feet. As Christians we are members of His body, seated positionally in the heavens with Him now (Ephesians 2:6). Whether we represent the soles of His feet or the hair on the top of His head, we are still positionally above anything placed underneath His feet.

With the ground rules in place, the rest of the meeting is basically a systematic mop up. I ask the counselee to pick the first two or three areas he would like us to check first. I ask him to choose those specific areas that represent the greatest problems.

Usually demons with the greater authority are overseeing those areas that represent greater problems. By going after the higher ranking spirits first you can shorten the process. When the leaders go, they take all those under their specific charge with them.

When I initially began working with demonized Christians I would have all the demons give their names. The list got long, and the lower ranking demons tried to protect those with higher rank. I eventually found out that by identifying the officers first you can avoid the games.

If the first area we are dealing with is fear, I will say something like this: "_____, we are going to deal with the area of fear because you told me it's a major problem. Before we confront demons you will need to confess any sin(s) and ask God to cancel any ground held by demons in this area of your life." The individual will then ask God to forgive him of the sin of fear that has dominated his life. It ultimately represents a lie that is a slap in the face of God because it denies His goodness and promise to always care for His children. Fear gives more credit to enemies who want to hurt God's children than it does to God who has promised to protect us.

After the person confesses this sin as thoroughly as he knows how, I ask him to pray that God would cancel any and all grounds demons might hold against him through this area. Confession brings cleansing to a specific area where the person has given ground to Satan. Canceling closes the door to the opportunity or foothold that the person has given over and that the demon has taken advantage of through unconfessed sin. With the sin forgiven and the ground divinely removed, demons are now unwanted squatters rather than invited or tolerated guests.

At this point I will command:

"If there are any demons working in _____
in the area of fear, we bind all of you together along
with all of your works and effects and command
that you come forward now."

"We now command that spirit holding highest
authority of all those bound and brought forward in
the area of fear to step up alone. We put a hedge of
thorns around you, above you and below you. You
will not be interfered with by anyone."

The initial questions I ask are specific, simple, straightforward and easy to remember. I am interested in identifying a demon's name, commissioning source, specific job, habitual lies and the ground it holds. Once the demonized person learns to recognize the demon's answers, usually described as a voice, words, thoughts, impressions or ideas that pop into his mind in direct response to the questions being addressed, the process goes much faster. I typically ask the individual to allow me to filter his thoughts by repeating to me, word for word, the voices, thoughts, words, ideas and so forth that he is hearing or thinking in response to the questions. Because I have gone though it enough times I can usually tell what is real and what is creative imagination.

Demons will respond to the questions addressed to them. But they will often try to confuse those involved in hopes of shutting down the entire process. Demons are reluctant to leave their assignments until they have completed their jobs for fear of retribution from those with higher authority in their chain of destruction. Their voices, suggestions and accusations are often so familiar that the counselee has learned to accept them, believing them his own thoughts.

If he doesn't hear any answers in response to a question, I ask him to simply tell me it is all quiet. When demons are present,

I have found it very typical for the person to first hear answers like, "_____, my name is _____. But you've made this all up in your head. Don't tell him that name because he'll think you're making this up. You'll look foolish."

First question. The first question I usually ask is: "In the name of the Lord Jesus Christ we have commanded that spirit holding the highest authority working in the area of fear in _____ to step forward alone. What is your name?"

If there are demons present, they will answer. Sometimes it is easy. The person will say, "Karl, the name _____ just came in my mind." When this happens I will say, "You have responded to the name _____. We bind you by that name, and upon command you will go to the pit bound by that name with all of your works and effects and all of your associates and their works and effects as well."

Second question. "In the name of the Lord Jesus Christ, who commissioned you in the work you are doing against _____?" The answer usually is Satan or some other similar title, i.e. Lucifer, The Dark Lord and so forth.

Third question. In the name of the Lord Jesus Christ, "What work have you been commissioned to do against _____?" The response to this is usually "To destroy him or to kill him."

The follow up question is: "In the name of the Lord Jesus Christ, by what means do you hope to destroy him?" The answers will vary, but if it is really a demon, the answer will have something to do with the work it is trying to accomplish.

Suicide. We tell her to take her own life. We make her feel worthless so she will give up. We are destroying her marriage by creating problems in her family etc.

Fourth Question. "In the name of the Lord Jesus Christ, what lies do you tell _____ on a habitual basis?"

We tell her that God will not protect her. We torment her with fear, and she believes us. We tell

*her she will get sick and die, and that her husband
does not really love her. We tell her she is going
crazy and that she is not really a Christian who is
going to heaven. You are ugly. You are fat. No one
likes you. You are always alone and always will be.
It is never going to change.*

The lies will consistently relate to the work they have been
commissioned to carry out.

Fifth question. The fifth and most important question is:
"In the name of the Lord Jesus Christ, *do you still hold any ground
against _____ that would keep you from leaving him upon
command?"* Whether the answer is "Yes" or "No," I will usually
test it against the white throne of God, at least at first.

I can't tell you why demons will always tell the truth when
asked if the answer they have given will stand as true before the
white throne of God. But I can tell you they will tell you the truth,
even if they lied and deceived earlier, probably testing you to see if
you know what you are doing. I asked the pastor who mentored me
in spiritual warfare deliverance ministry why lying demons
immediately came clean when we challenged their answers before
the white throne of God. He simply told me that in his sixty years
of working in this area of ministry, demons came clean when he
placed this question before them. I still don't know the why, but I
too can tell you, speaking pragmatically, that it works. I will ask
Jesus about it when I meet Him, but until then I will continue to
ask this question when an answer just doesn't ring true to me.

If the answer is "Yes," I will proceed. If the response is,
"No, it won't stand as truth," then I don't move past that point. It's
not unusual for a follow-up comment like, "I was hoping to create
confusion so that I could stay longer."

Once the answer is "we hold no more ground" or
something similar, you have everything you need to command it to
leave. Once the ground is gone, the demon will leave upon
command. Until you deal with the specific ground held it will not
go.

I have found that when demons give arrogant answers it's usually because they either don't think you know what you're doing or they don't think you will uncover the ground they hold against the person. They will also respond arrogantly if the person you are working with has a weak will and the demons think they can scare or shame him into shutting down the process through intimidation and/or confusing answers. They will frequently say things to the person like: "You'll never get us all." "We're powerful, and your faith is pitiful." "If you make us go we will come back and get you and your loved ones." "If you tell him all the ground we hold he will not respect you."

Another thing I found is that when they hold the area of ancestral sin they are certain you will never uncover it. They are confident they will remain free to continue their destructive work. I now have the person take care of the ancestral issues up front with the initial confession and canceling of sin, just in case it is an issue.

> *Lord Jesus if there are any spirits who have anything to do with me, body, soul or spirit because of ancestral sin, I ask you to please forgive this sin(s) and cancel any ground held against me because of ancestral sin. I want nothing to do with ancestral sin and give the entire area to you.*

If you take care of the issue of ancestral sin and ground at the start, it will not come up again. If you don't cover it and there are demons that hold ancestral ground, they will play games until you finally get around to challenging this area.

Demons are very predictable. They even seem sloppy at times. I believe this is because they so seldom run into someone who knows how to effectively deal with them that they think they are safe. You can often use their arrogance against them.

On some occasions when asking the first question about the spirit holding highest authority in a particular area to identify itself, the demon will try to mock God and to take control of the process. I have received this type of answer:

We are not here. No one is working in that area. This is not necessary.

The first time that happened I had to keep from laughing. The brother I was working with burst out in laughter saying, "This idiot just told me it is not there."

Two things are left to bring this first area (fear) to closure. You must command the demons to leave and ask the Holy Spirit to fill every area (room) the demons have vacated. I have the counselee repeat a command with me. I remind him that we are commanding as victors, not asking or pleading as victims.

> *In the name of the Lord Jesus Christ we command*
> *(fill in the demon's name), to leave _____*
> *with all of your works and effects and all of your*
> *associates and their works and effects and go to the*
> *pit right now. We command this in the name of the*
> *Lord Jesus Christ who is the King of Kings, the*
> *Lord of Lords and my Savior. Amen.*

After you pray this, the person will then ask the Holy Spirit to fill and control the areas just vacated. Matthew 12:25–45 indicates that after binding and expelling a demon, it is necessary to fill the room(s) it has worked in or attached to with someone stronger than it. Who is stronger than God? No one! The Holy Spirit longs to completely fill and control every believer. When we allow the Holy Spirit to fill and control our entire lives, it is as though we have hung out a sign for passing demons to read that says "No Vacancy."

Attempting to command demons to leave a non-Christian is risky for at least two reasons. First, a non-Christian has no authority base in Christ to stand on. Without confessing sin and canceling ground, demons will not usually leave. Before a person can expect Jesus Christ to stand up as his advocate (defense lawyer), Christ must become his personal Savior. Second, when demons leave a person without Christ the result is a clean tidy room with a "Vacancy" sign. If God doesn't move in and fill that room or house, who will show up again for round two? You are right. Therefore, the first decision a non-Christian needs to make in confronting demons is to become a true Christian.

The reason I referred to this process as a systematic mop up is because after we deal with each issue completely, I repeat this same process for each remaining area of concern. The last area dealt with is commanding the highest ranking spirit other than the Holy Spirit to come forward. If anything is left, we can deal with it in the same way.

When the entire process is complete I ask the individual to do three things.

1   Practice keeping short accounts with sin. When there is no unconfessed sin there is no corresponding ground to give up.

One of the things I have heard many times from those trying to disparage this type of ministry service is that the people who believe they are free of demons will become casual with sin and convinced that everything and everyone else has demonic problems, too.

Once again, if the repetition can make something true then this must be so, at least in some circles. But I have not found this the case. The people I know who have worked through this process have learned that playing with sin isn't worth it. They want to stay away from the edge and not make a game out of seeing how close they can walk to sin before they fall in again.

Although they may have heard the need for holiness preached since they were children, they now receive it with respect rather than familiarity. The world, the flesh and the devil are all real enemies. We must deal with all three and not one at the expense of the others. A person who has survived the fire is usually more careful around the flames than someone who doesn't think it will burn him.

2   Consistently practice offensive prayer.

When was the last time you read through the Psalms? As you were reading did you ever notice how many times David prayed offensively as well as defensively? David does ask God to be his strong fortress and to hide him. (See Psalm 27) But he also asks God to destroy those trying to destroy him. He asks God to catch his adversaries in the very snares they set for him. When he asks God to drop his enemies into the pits they have dug for him, he is not praying defensively. I was out of Bible school and seminary before I ever recognized this truth. (See Psalm 35:1–8.)

Demons are stronger and smarter than we are. But we have an advocate who is infinitely stronger and smarter than they are. In Christ we are the victors. We must not try to stand alone against demons. I encourage believers to call upon God not only to protect them from evil (defensive prayer) but also to expose and tear down those trying to destroy His Children (offensive prayer). He will faithfully answer this type of prayer. Alone, we are no match for demons. But we are not alone. And demons are no match for the One committed to protecting us.

Read through the Psalms again and put a "D" by every defensive prayer you find. Put an "O" by every offensive prayer you find. I think you will probably be amazed and a bit surprised at the results. I sure was!

Maybe Paul was giving us a hint about the power of focused prayer in relationship to spiritual warfare when he told the believers in Ephesians 6:18, *"With all prayer and petition pray at all times in the Spirit, and with this in view, be on the alert with all perseverance and petition for all the saints."* This command comes after the entire section detailing putting on the full armor of God, not before. There are many good Psalms illustrating offensive prayer, but Psalms 35 and 83 are two of my favorites.

3   Read your Bibles and apply what you learn.

Matthew 4:1–12 records Satan's temptation of Jesus. It is interesting to notice how Jesus referred to Scripture with each of Satan's temptations. It is very difficult to respond correctly to error if we don't know what is true.

This is one more area where we have the privilege of being able to follow our example for life and godliness, Jesus Christ. I am convinced that demons have more respect and fear of the Word of God than most Christians. When I run into an occasional demon who is acting particularly stubborn or arrogant I will start reading from the Bible. I will usually switch off with the counselee, and we will read chapter after chapter. Besides annoying the demon, it will also encourage the afflicted Christian. It will just be a matter of time before that demon will begin to ask us to please stop reading from that book with a promise to cooperate as commanded.

I have also learned that an appeal to the Holy Spirit for His powerful intercession against an arrogant demon who is attempting to step outside the ground rules brings the same result, only much quicker. Demons are no match for God, and they will comply quickly when you ask for the Holy Spirit's active intercession. *You have not because....*

On a few occasions individuals have called and asked if they could return because they feared we missed something. A follow-up appointment usually didn't take more than thirty minutes. The counselee understands what to do and how the process works. Normally, however, this isn't necessary. And if people somehow open or reopen a foothold, they now know how to deal with the sin and ground themselves right away. It is exciting to watch God work in their lives as they learn to walk in victory on top of hell's army rather than experience mental and emotional torment beneath it.

The goal, or at least my goal, is for each person I work with to understand that because of their authority in the Lord Jesus Christ, they no longer need me or anyone else to guide them through this process. The same God who lives in me lives in them, and He is more than willing to protect His children. I have watched passive, fearful, defeated Christians become bold soldiers who learn to quickly resist the devil rather than to entertain his accusations, play his games, or run. It's a joy to lock arms with brothers and sisters in Christ who realize we are more than conquerors who don't have to run from a defeated enemy.

9

Demonic Warfare:

Common Questions

People have repeatedly asked me to answer a handful of questions concerning spiritual warfare. Over the years these questions have changed very little whether asked by friends at church, students at seminary or lay leaders and pastors of local churches. I don't pretend to have all the answers to all of these questions. Humanistically speaking it would be helpful if the Bible had included a systematic "how to" book on spiritual warfare, much like it does salvation in the book of Romans. But that single systematic book of the Bible on spiritual warfare does not exist. God in His providence chose to sprinkle the topic of spiritual warfare throughout His written word just like other topics we profess without hesitation or apology. For instance, we don't have a single book or even a chapter clearly addressing the topics of heaven or the Trinity. He expects us to do our homework.

People have told me that the lack of systematic teaching in the New Testament on the subject of spiritual warfare is an indication of its apparent lack of priority from God's viewpoint.

If God had wanted Christians aggressively involved in spiritual warfare and confronting demons He would have provided clear, systematic instructions on how to do this, rather than force us to pick and choose information and principles throughout the New Testament.

I suppose that's one way to look at this situation. However, I would like to suggest another explanation.

First, the New Testament has more written in it concerning spiritual warfare in general, and demonic bondage and deliverance specifically, than its readers often admit if they are willing to approach the subject without assuming their conclusions. Second, as mentioned earlier, there are a number of topics we accept and teach as foundational to the Christian faith that lack clear systematic instruction in either the Old or New Testaments.

Take the Trinity for instance. What would happen if we applied this same standard to the topic of the Trinity?

Is God one? Yes, He is (Deuteronomy 6:4, Mark 12:29). But isn't it possible to identify three different persons in Scripture as God? Yes it is. (*The Father*: 2 Peter 1:17; *The Son*: Mark 14:60–65, John 8:58, 10:30–33, Philippians 2:5–6, Colossians 2:9, Titus 2:13, 2 Peter 1:1, Revelation 1:8, 17, 18, 22:13, 16; *The Holy Spirit*: Acts 5:1–5.)

Three distinct persons—but in essence only one God. Both are true. Does Scripture support the doctrine of the Trinity, and has orthodox Christianity made it the historic doctrinal teaching for nearly two millennia concerning the nature of the Godhead? The answer to both questions is "Yes." Can one single verse, one systematic chapter, or an entire book of the Bible dedicated to explaining the subject easily explain or maintain this doctrine? The answer to these questions is "No."

But if it is a priority to God, wouldn't He have provided clear, systematic instruction on something as important as His own nature? This question assumes that there is a direct correlation between the number of times a subject is mentioned in the Bible and the value that should be assigned to it. As I have already demonstrated, this is neither a safe or biblically based assumption.

Christians need to thank God that the disciples and Ante-Nicene church fathers had more concern about being Biblically correct than appearing politically, scholastically or culturally correct to their peers. Paul reminded the Corinthians that the subject of the resurrection was a stumbling block to the Jewish mind and absurd nonsense to the Greek philosophers. Faithful Christians like Paul continued to preach the resurrection regardless of the reception they knew their message would receive. Christians in the West do not choose to live and speak as courageously in the face of political, social and physical opposition!

Many ancient and modern-day cults exist primarily because of confusion over this very issue and its apparent ambiguities in Scripture. Apparently God didn't intend for Christians to make the number of verses or books in the Bible dedicated to a particular topic a litmus test for the priority He places upon it.

Is it possible that the reason verses on spiritual warfare appear less systematically than some would like is because the Jews of Jesus' and Paul's day were so familiar with the subject that they didn't assume it necessary to write position papers justifying a common practice? When the Jewish leaders accused Jesus of casting out demons by the power of the devil, He responded by asking them by what authority and power their sons cast out demons (Matthew 12:27). There was no denial from the religious leaders about their sons' involvement in this type of work. The point of the confrontation was not over the practice of deliverance ministry, but the source of the power and authority Jesus exercised to accomplish the job.

The sons of Sceva didn't draw particular attention for attempting to cast out demons. They became a focal point of attention when they tried to confront demons in their own authority rather than in Christ's (Acts 19:13–17). Again, the issue was not the practice of deliverance but the authority behind it.

In Mark 9:38–39 and Luke 9:49, the Apostle John informed Jesus that someone was casting out demons in His name.

> *Teacher, we saw someone casting out demons in*
> *Your name, and we tried to hinder him because he*
> *was not following us.*

Was the issue once again the authority and association by which they were doing this or a particular problem with the practice of deliverance in general? If the issue was the practice rather than the group association, one would suspect that Jesus might have expressed more surprise.

> *He was doing what? What in the world was he*
> *trying to do? People are going to mistake us for*
> *Pharisees and their sons. If I wanted him to do that*
> *I would have included specific teaching in the*
> *Sermon on the Mount. I don't want anything to do*
> *with this type of emotional extremism. Tell him to*
> *knock it off before I turn him into a salt lick.*

Look at Jesus' actual response to John concerning this matter.

> *Do not hinder him, for there is no one who shall*
> *perform a miracle in My name, and be able soon*
> *afterwards to speak evil of Me. For whoever gives*
> *you a cup of water to drink because of your name as*
> *followers of Christ, truly I say to you, he shall not*
> *lose his reward.*

Apparently orthodox Jews or first century Christians didn't consider exorcism, or deliverance, unique or an oddity. The only serious questions Scripture consistently raises seem related to the source of the power or authority exercised in the practice.

Second Corinthians 2:10–11 supports the explanation that the lack of systematic instruction regarding spiritual warfare could stem from its familiarity rather than its obscurant practice. Paul wrote:

> *But whom you forgive anything, I forgive also; for*
> *indeed what I have forgiven, if I have forgiven*
> *anything, I did it for your sakes in the presence of*
> *Christ, in order that no advantage be taken of us by*
> *Satan; **for we are not ignorant of his schemes.***

How many Christians do you know today who could make that same claim with any confidence concerning their understanding of Satan's schemes? We typically spend more time and energy trying to ignore or deny Satan's schemes than we do explaining them. Individuals who argue against the need for a more comprehensive approach to training on the world, the flesh, and particularly the devil, because of a presumed lack of Scripture to support the practice, are often guilty of arguing from silence and begging the question. They assume their conclusion in their presuppositions. In logic we consider this faulty reasoning. In warfare it is a dangerous invitation to receive a spiritual beating.

I have been told that Christians can be oppressed and non-Christians possessed. Is this true?

Yes, this statement as typically defined through the oppression/possession paradigm is true as far as it goes. The problem is that it does not go far enough. We find an easy way to remember how to explain the concept of oppression for believers in Ephesians 6:10–18 and Revelation 12:10. John states that the devil accuses the brethren on a daily basis.

> *For the accuser of our brethren has been thrown down, who accuses them before God day and night.*

Paul indicates in Ephesians 6:16 that Satan and his demonic host shoot flaming missiles at Christians.

> *In addition to all, taking up the shield of faith with which you will be able to extinguish all the flaming missiles of the evil one.*

It is my opinion that the accusations of Revelation 12 and the flaming missiles of Ephesians 6 are one and the same thing. Both represent supernatural oppression directed primarily against Christians.

The flaming missiles and the accusations are both external in the nature of their attacks. We can use the blood of the lamb, the word of our testimony and the shield of faith to take care of both of these problems.

Remember, the word translated "possession" Biblically and etymologically in fact has more to do with varying degrees of internal control than with actual ownership. Oppression represents external temptations and propositions to sin while demonic possession deals more with internal control and mental, emotional or physical domination. Is it possible for Satan to totally dominate and control a non-Christian? Yes, it is. Is it possible for Satan or his demons to possess a Christian? If we understand the word "possession" to mean complete control or total mental, emotional, physical and spiritual domination over a Christian, then "no," it is not possible for Satan to possess a true Christian.

If it isn't possible for the devil or demons to possess a true Christian, then why does this book indicate that the people you have worked with are demonized Christians? I'm confused by what you are saying. Can demons possess Christians or not?

This question is important. (I have already addressed it in Chapters One and Six.) However, it doesn't have to be as confusing as it may seem at first glance. The confusion over this issue usually lies in the "oppression" *or* "possession" paradigm through which people typically approach this question.

Do you remember that I said the "oppression" for Christians and "possession" for non-Christians was accurate as far as it went, but that it didn't go far enough? It's time to explain the qualifier in this statement.

As long as we frame the question of the demonization of Christians in the traditional oppression/possession paradigm it's easy to give it a clear, commanding, simple answer: Demons can oppress but not possess Christians. If a person indicates his struggles are more than external demonic oppression, and assuming the issues in question are real and not mental or physiological, then that person must not be a true Christian. Why? Because the traditional either/or oppression/possession paradigm says so.

What if that paradigm is wrong? What if we can demonstrate a real difference not only between oppression and possession, but also between "possession" as traditionally defined and demonization? The assumption in the old paradigm is that all demonization represents total demonic possession and that Christians can't be possessed. What happens to the traditional paradigm if it is possible for a Christian to be demonized, although never absolutely and totally controlled or dominated by demonic spirits?

Either it is oppression or it is possession is a much easier way to discuss a topic most Christians are both unfamiliar with and uncomfortable explaining. The problem is that the simplicity of the either/or paradigm doesn't fully account for Bible verses that allow for the demonization of Christians. It also doesn't account for the testimonies of Christian laymen and leaders in North America and around the world whose struggles certainly appear more severe than oppression but that fall short of total demonic control and domination.

Missionaries have indicated for many years that they have had to deal with genuine believers who still struggled with demonic bondage. Dick Hillis and Ed Murphy of Overseas Crusade have both shared experiences of this nature in a straightforward, non-exploitive format. The late Merrill Unger acknowledged that the consistent testimonies of trusted missionaries were one reason he changed his position on this issue. In his book *Biblical Demonology* published in 1952, he wrote that true Christians could not be demonized. In 1960 in his classic work *Demons in our World Today*, he reversed his position.

These men are not alone in their thinking. Faculty members have existed in solidly Evangelical schools who shared the same conviction regarding the possibility of the demonization of Christians—schools like Talbot Seminary, Western Seminary, Dallas Theological Seminary, Trinity Evangelical Divinity School, Moody Bible Institute, Wheaton College, Multnomah School of the Bible, and no doubt other respected Christian schools, too.

If someone wants to insist on maintaining the oppression/possession paradigm approach to this question as though it is sacrosanct, then I guess that settles the question, and a lot of Christian men we thought we could trust and respect have apparently lost their minds over the subject of spiritual warfare. If though we allow paradigms to shift without accusing someone of abandoning his faith, then maybe there is still room in the choir for one more voice and verse on this song. But we must decide to keep this discussion centered in the Scripture rather than in ideological position papers and insist that our positions be able to pass reality tests with the people we are attempting to minister to.

How and where do demons attach themselves to a believer?

The simple answer is that I do not know exactly how or where demons attach themselves to a Christian. I do not know if they attach themselves internally or externally. What I do know though is that demons are potentially able to control a place, a space or a territory in a believer's life because Ephesians 4:27 states this is the case without equivocation.

Here are two illustrations that explain how this phenomenon may occur.

First, have you ever swum in a body of water that contained leeches? If you do, how surprised should you be if one or more of them attaches themselves to your body and begins to suck out your life blood until you remove them? This possibility may seem repulsive to someone who has never swum with leeches, but the aversion does not negate the possibility, as offensive as it may seem.

The bottom line is this. If you are foolish enough to swim with leeches, don't be surprised to find them attached to your body. Are they inside or outside of your body? Leeches attach themselves on the outside of your body, but this does not keep them from draining your blood as long as you allow them to.

Demons are leeches that attempt to destroy your life by sucking out your life blood and ability to serve the Lord Jesus Christ. They have no right to your life if you are a Christian, but if you are foolish enough to swim with them, they will attach themselves to your body, and they will remain there until you exercise your authority to remove them.

Can we compare a demon's ability to attach itself to a believer to a leech in a swimming pond? Yes, I think this is possible, and it may illustrate how this can happen. Do I know for certain how demons attach themselves to believers and control a place, a space or a territory in their lives? No, I do not. But I do not know how God is going to change my physical body in a moment of time or what it will look like after this happens either. The Apostle Paul, writing in 1 Corinthians 15, says he did not know exactly how this is going to happen or what we will look like. However, our inability to explain the what's and how's of our resurrection bodies right now does not negate the fact that we are going to receive them as promised in 1 Corinthians 15.

Second, imagine a house lit up on a dark lonely night. The more rooms in the house that have lights on, the brighter the house will appear to a lost stranger. On the other hand, the more rooms that are dark, the less contrast that house will have in the darkness and the less likely a stranger will see it as a source of safety and shelter.

Can the house's landlord decide to allow a stranger to rent a room in the house? Yes! If the renter turns out to be an honest, helpful handyman the landlord may even extend more privileges to him or offer a long term lease. If the renter ends up being a dishonest person who deliberately destroys the room he rented, the landlord may evict him. Does the renter being honest or dishonest have anything to do with who legally owns the house? No, it does not.

Is it possible for a bad renter to intimidate the house's landlord into letting him stay, even though he wants him out? Yes. Doesn't the landlord have the right and authority to remove a bad renter if he chooses to do so? Yes again. If the landlord, motivated by fear, decides to tolerate a bad renter and allow him to stay, whose fault is it if that renter remains and continues to destroy the house? If the renter knows he has successfully intimidated the landlord do you suppose he will be content to remain confined in the one room he has rented?

If the landlord fails to exercise his authority, how long do you suppose it will take before that renter tries to take over the bathroom, kitchen and recreation room, besides the bedroom he has already destroyed? Do any of these circumstances affect in any way who legally owns that house? No, they do not. The real issue is why the landlord would continue to tolerate the bad renter, not who is the owner of the house.

What do houses, lights, landlords, owners and renters have to do with a question about demonization and Christians? Plenty! As Christians, our lives represent houses (or lights) that should shine brightly in the night to contrast with the darkness surrounding us (Philippians 2:14–15). We are supposed to provide the good news of safety and shelter for weary strangers who are lost in the night and looking for help. There is a direct correlation between the number of brightly lit rooms in our house and the number of needy individuals who will seek and find help there.

When Jesus Christ becomes our Savior, He wants complete control of every room in our house. As our Savior, He is the rightful owner of our house. He paid the debts held against our house, and as the new owner He has the right to do anything with it that He chooses. When we fail to yield control of our life's rooms to Him, we are effectively turning out the lights in that room. Darkened rooms do not jeopardize our salvation because they do not determine who owns the house, but they certainly limit the scope and effectiveness of our witness to people stumbling and groping in the darkness around us.

Although Jesus is the legal owner of our house, He allows us the privilege and responsibility of being the landlord. He has given us back our house on loan. We have the authority and ability to sublease rooms in our house, even though we do not own the house. The only rooms available for rent are the ones we have refused to turn over to the lordship of Christ. When we turn lights out through sin, we essentially place a vacancy sign outside that reads, "Rooms for Rent." Demonic spirits are more than willing to answer the ad. And once they have permission to rent one room, they will aggressively and simultaneously attempt to take control of other rooms while inviting relatives to move in with them.

Whether the lights are on or off, our serving as stewards or landlords has nothing to do with who owns the house. Allowing demonic renters to move in and trash their rooms does not affect our house's ownership either. Landlords and renters can live in the same house at the same time without affecting the building's legal ownership. The issue at stake is our stewardship as the delegated spokespersons for the owner, not His ownership. Landlords have the authority to evict bad renters when they realize they have made a mistake, assuming they have the courage to exercise their legal rights.

When we realize we have made a terrible mistake allowing demonic spirits to rent rooms, we can admit our mistake, confess our sin to the owner and ask Him to use His power and authority to remove the renters. He is glad to help. He ultimately is more concerned about the well being of our house than we are because He paid a great price for it.

If we choose to ignore the problems demonic renters create, hoping to hide the matter from the owner or thinking that they will volunteer to just go away on their own initiative, it's only a matter of time before things go from bad to worse. Demonic renters, like most bad renters, will not volunteer to leave a place they can call home unless forced to do so.

Bad renters can't keep broken windows and fences, holes in walls, a leaky roof and plugged sewer lines secret from an involved owner very long. A responsible owner will confront the landlord and let him know that he has noticed his irresponsibility. He may give a repentant landlord another chance. Realizing the grace and forgiveness the owner has extended him, the landlord may actually turn out more discerning, faithful, grateful, watchful and harder to fool than someone who has never encountered troublesome renters.

If the owner doesn't sense any change in his landlord's heart and attitude, it's possible that he may decide his representative is costing him too much and remove him from his responsibilities. He may choose to give his steward a job with fewer responsibilities and less opportunity for rewards or he may decide to give him an early retirement, minus the gold watch, balloons and cake. The joy of a retirement party for faithful service will turn into the shame of forfeited future rewards because of divided loyalties and irresponsible behavior.

I have shared this extended example because it deals directly with the question under consideration: **How can demons control areas of a person's life and yet not own that person?** This question can also be presented as a declaratory statement rather than a question; it usually sounds something like this:

> *The Bible says it isn't possible for God and demons to own the same person or share the same space. God is holy and will have nothing to do with evil. Therefore, it is not possible for God and demons to exist in the same person.*

There's nothing wrong with this conclusion if the premises are correct. But are they correct? It's true that God and demons can't own the same person. Does owning, having access or renting space, necessarily mean the same thing? A renter can have access to a house and not own it. An owner can have access to his home and not be a renter. Many Christians assume that comments like: *God and demons cannot own the same person, and, God and evil cannot share the same space* are synonymous statements. They are not.

Our world is fallen. Man is fallen. The things of God are foolish to the natural man. He cannot understand them. If it is true that God will not share space with evil or a demon, then how can God be involved with His creation? If God is omnipresent there isn't anywhere we can't ultimately find His presence or influence.

If the *not sharing space with evil* statement is true, then what do we do with Romans 7:15–25 and Galatians 5:17? Paul identifies our flesh as an evil entity within our members that is at war with the Spirit who resides in us as believers (1 Corinthians 3:16; 6:19–20). Although the cross of Christ crucified our old man, it did not eradicate our flesh. Its legal hold over us as slaves of sin is broken. But this does not mean it doesn't exist. According to Scripture the world has also been crucified to us and us to it. But what Christian is going to say that the temptations and propositions of the world don't exist or affect us? Why would James (James 4:4) and John (1 John 2:15–17) admonish Christians to stop loving the world if crucifixion means eradication? It makes no sense to tell believers to quit loving something that no longer exists.

As Christians we no longer have to be slaves of sin. This is true whether the solicitations enticing us to sin are sociological, physiological or supernatural in origin. But if we choose to obey the world, the flesh or the devil rather than the Lord Jesus Christ, we can certainly become enslaved to any of them, even if we are blood-bought, pew-jumping, praise-singing, truth–speaking, born-again Christians.

Since Scripture is very clear that God is willing to share space in our bodies with our flesh, which is evil, what reason, logic or revelation compels us to believe that a demon could not also share this same space?

But I've always heard—I've always been taught—I've always understood—that God and demons would not share space. Jesus and Paul taught this, didn't they? My mentor teaches this, and now I do, too. Don't all serious Christians agree with this teaching?

No, all serious Christians do not agree with this thinking. I grew up hearing that the Bible says *God helps those who help themselves*. I heard, I was taught and I always understood do not make this statement Biblical or true. One of my humanities professors told our class that he heard, was taught and understood that the Bible said the Earth is flat. He had a habit of ridiculing Christians in his classes. I asked him if he could show us exactly where the Bible said the Earth was flat. He could not and embarrassed himself in the process of trying to make fun of Christians in general and Christianity specifically, both of which he despised with open contempt.

We of all people must check the Scripture to see what it says, just as Paul commended the Bereans in Acts 17:11 or as he commanded Timothy in 2 Timothy 2:15.

> *Now these were more noble-minded than those in Thessalonica, for they received the word with eagerness, examining the Scriptures daily, to see whether these things were so.* Acts 17:11

> *Be diligent to present yourself approved to God as a workman who does not need to be ashamed, handling accurately the word of truth.* 2 Timothy 2:15

Where does the Bible specifically say that God and a demon cannot have access to the same person? People often use 2 Corinthians 6:14–17 as a proof text to support the position that demons cannot infest, invade, control or demonize a true Christian. What does this passage actually say?

> *Do not be bound together with unbelievers; for what partnership have righteousness and lawlessness, or what fellowship has light with darkness? Or what harmony has Christ with Belial, or what has a believer in common with an unbeliever? Or what agreement has the temple of God with idols? For we are the temple of the living God; just as God said, " I WILL DWELL IN THEM AND WALK AMONG THEM; AND I WILL BE THEIR GOD, AND THEY SHALL BE MY PEOPLE. THEREFORE, COME OUT FROM THEIR MIDST AND BE SEPARATE," says the Lord. "AND DO NOT TOUCH WHAT IS UNCLEAN; And I will welcome you."*

Is this passage actually an emphatic teaching that demons cannot demonize a Christian or is this passage an exhortation from Paul to the Corinthian believers, challenging them to quit doing something they are already doing, i.e. still living like non-Christians even though they profess themselves Christians?

Apparently the brethren were still allowing their most intimate relationships and associations to occur with people who hate God.

As Christians, we need to walk in a different direction than we were traveling as non-Christians. We must follow Christ. Following dead idols may be part of our old lives, but as followers of the Lord Jesus Christ our ultimate loyalty should be to Him, and our closest relationships should be with the people who profess to love and serve Him, too.

Didn't Paul share this same basic message with this same group of people in an earlier letter? He said:

> *"And such were some of you; but you were washed, but you were sanctified, but you were justified in the name of the Lord Jesus Christ, and in the Spirit of our God. All things are lawful for me, but not all things are profitable. All things are lawful for me but I will not be mastered by anything."* 1 Corinthians 6:11-12

*Such as some of you were...*you used to live in darkness, now you live in light. You used to worship idols, now you worship the one true God. Jesus Christ has changed your life, so start living your profession, guard your relationships and walk your talk. It is as though Paul is saying, "When you became a Christian you accepted Jesus as your Lord and Savior. Why in the world are you still living more like unbelievers than believers? A right relationship with God should produce a changed lifestyle. Wake up!"

Some may object that a real Christian would never be willing to live with one foot serving heaven while the other foot is playing games with the world, the flesh or the devil. Reread Paul's evaluation of some of the carnal Christians living in Corinth.

> *And I, brethren, could not speak to you as to spiritual men, but as to men of flesh, as to babes in Christ. I gave you milk to drink, not solid food; for you were not yet able to receive it. Indeed, even now you are not yet able, for you are fleshly. For since*

there is jealousy and strife among you, are you not fleshly, and are you not walking like mere men? 1 Corinthians 3:1–3

If you still want to insist that you always follow Jesus Christ as Savior and Lord, never hitting any sin bumps in the process, I would like the opportunity to speak, uncensored, with those who know you best—possibly your children, parents, spouse, best friends, neighbors and employer. Will they agree with your self-evaluation regarding the consistency of your obedience to Jesus Christ? Reality tests, as well as the Scripture (i.e. 1 John 1:8–2:1) argue convincingly that all Christians still battle with sin's solicitations in an active way.

So what's the point? Second Corinthians 6 isn't talking about the ontology of God or man nor the possible demonized relationship between demons and man. It is Paul's exhortation for Christians to live as new creatures with changed lives. The use of this verse as a proof text to oppose the possibility of Christians being demonized is a disgraceful manipulation of this text. It is the best that is available for those promoting that particular position though.

Acts 5:1–6 records an instructive story about two born again believers named Ananias and Sapphira. This incident relates directly to questions involving Christians, demonic control, deception, personal responsibility and God's opinion of the value He places on his children promoting and practicing honesty both publicly and privately.

> *But a man named Ananias, with his wife Sapphira, sold a piece of property, and kept back some of the price for himself, with his wife's full knowledge, and bringing a portion of it, he laid it at the apostles' feet.*

> *But Peter said, "Ananias, why has Satan filled your heart to lie to the Holy Spirit and to keep back some of the price of the land? While it remained unsold, did it not remain your own? And after it was sold,*

> *was it not under your control? Why is it that you*
> *have conceived this deed in your heart? You have*
> *not lied to men but to God."*
>
> *And as he heard these words, Ananias fell down and*
> *breathed his last; and great fear came over all who*
> *heard of it.*

Ananias and Sapphira sold a piece of property and gave part of the proceeds to the Apostles to help other believers who were struggling in poverty as a result of their commitment to Christ. The particular problem confronting this couple was that they lied about how much money they sold the property for and how much of that amount they were dedicating to God for benevolence work.

In confronting Ananias, Peter said that the lie he had just told was not to men but to God. Peter asked Ananias, *why has Satan filled your heart to lie to the Holy Spirit, and to keep back some of the price of the land?* The lie this Christian couple agreed to tell cost both of them their lives. I can only guess that the apparent severity of this judgment was God's way of saying that He would not tolerate *deception* or *pretense* in His church. The Pharisees had already turned people away from God through both of these destructive practices, and God did not want either to gain a foothold in the body of Christ.

What does this story have to do with the question about the possibility of God and demons both having the ability to control a Christian's mind and subsequent actions? There is no reason from the text to assume Ananias and Sapphira were anything but genuine Christians, struggling with battles from the world, the flesh and the devil. Perhaps they were insecure and shortsighted, but they were still Christians—members of the Jerusalem church recognized and known by name.

Peter indicated that Satan had filled their hearts. The word translated "filled" in this text, *eplerosen*, is from the same verb root (*plerao*) also used in Ephesians 5:18, which commands believers to be "filled" with the Holy Spirit, *plerousthe*.

Apparently, to whatever degree the Holy Spirit can fill or control a believer who is walking obediently, Satan or one of his demons can fill or control a believer who is walking in disobedience. Do we change the meaning and obvious implication of a word simply because it doesn't agree with our subjective theological suppositions and makes us uncomfortable? Or do we allow Scripture's etymology, context and interpretation to speak for itself, regardless of whose personal position it challenges?

Does Jesus Christ come into the heart of a Christian upon conversion? Yes, He does. Will God ever leave or forsake his children? No, He won't. If Jesus comes into our heart at conversion, then Jesus was in Ananias' heart. But Peter, inspired by the Holy Spirit, said that Satan filled Ananias' heart. Was Peter lying or was he just mistaken about Satan filling Ananias' heart? Did Jesus lie about never leaving us or forsaking us? If neither Jesus nor the Holy Spirit would lie, then both God and Satan were working in the heart of Ananias at the same time.

If I am committed, a priori, to the notion that God and Satan cannot share a place or space regardless of what Scripture seems to indicate, then am I prepared to reject the inspired language of the New Testament for my presuppositions? Should I adjust my presuppositions for Scripture or Scripture for my presuppositions?

Ephesians 1:13–14 clearly states that God sealed us with the Holy Spirit and gave us a new divine nature when we believed. Acts 5 and Ephesians 5 are just as clear that we have the privilege and responsibility for making choices every day that determine whether we willingly yield our mind to Holy Spirit or demonic control. How we must break the heart of God when we deliberately choose to treat His great sacrifice with indifference or contempt by trading the applause of God for the applause of man.

God has given Christians great privilege as members of the body of Christ. But with this privilege, there is also great responsibility to which God holds us accountable. To whom much is given, much is required! Sounds familiar doesn't it? When we choose to allow the Holy Spirit to control our thinking and actions we honor God. When we allow demonic spirits to control our thinking and actions we shame God. Obedience to God will produce an eternal reward (1 Cor.3:12–14). Disobedience will produce discipline for certain (Heb.12:9–12), and as Ananias and Sapphira found out it can even produce death (Acts 5:5–10).

Paul warns the Corinthians in 2 Corinthians 11:1–4 to quit **preaching** a different Jesus, **receiving** a different spirit and **accepting** a different gospel. Paul had betrothed the Corinthians to Christ, and they were following Jesus in pure devotion. Paul feared that as the serpent deceived Eve by his craftiness, that they too were being led astray in their minds from following Christ.

Is there any serious argument that Paul was addressing true Christians in 2 Corinthians 11:3? No! Is it true that all true Christians have the Holy Spirit? Yes! Romans 8:9 states:

> *However, you are not in the flesh but in the Spirit, if indeed the Spirit of God dwells in you. But if anyone does not have the Spirit of Christ, he does not belong to Him.*

The Corinthians were true Christians who had already received the Holy Spirit (1 Corinthians 12:13). Yet they are perplexing Paul with their willingness to preach a different Jesus, receive a different spirit and accept a different gospel. If they already had the Holy Spirit, what types of spirits were they receiving that concerned Paul so much? Demons? What other kinds of spirits are there?

Paul is clear that the one leading them astray was the same one who led Eve astray in the garden. The battleground in both cases was in their minds. God and Satan both have access to a believer's mind. And unless someone wants to argue that God would break His word and leave a Christian, it appears that God and Satan have the ability to share the same space at the same time—first the heart, now the mind.

In Luke 13:10–17 Jesus responds to the hypocrisy of the religious leaders who were upset with Him for healing a woman on the Sabbath. Verse 16 identifies the person Jesus healed as "a daughter of Abraham." The Bible typically reserves this term for the true children of the faith of Abraham. Unless one wants to argue against its normal usage, it appears she was a true believer who had placed her trust in the promised Messiah. The relevant point in this discussion is that verse 11 says that a spirit caused her sickness of eighteen years. Jesus states in verse 16 that Satan had bound this woman for eighteen years, and that it was right for Him to release her from her bondage on the Sabbath.

The Pharisees chose to argue the point. Jesus called them hypocrites for treating their animals with more care than a daughter of Abraham whom they were supposed to love. The point? Once again, we see a story that seems to indicate that it is possible for a demonic spirit to afflict a true child of God in a manner that goes far beyond the way we generally see oppression explained.

In 2 Corinthians 12:1–10, Paul writes about an experience he had when he was caught up into the third heaven. He explains that the event was so glorious that it was necessary for God to allow affliction so that he would not be overcome with pride. Concerning this affliction Paul wrote:

> *And because of the surpassing greatness of the revelations, for this reason, to keep me from exalting myself, there was given me a thorn in the flesh, a messenger of Satan to buffet me—to keep me from exalting myself!*

What was Paul's thorn in the flesh? Scholars speculate on this question, but no one knows for sure. Who was Satan's messenger sent as a thorn in Paul's flesh? A demon seems a reasonable assumption from a plain, literal understanding of the text, unless that possibility is rejected a priori because it so offends a person that he allows his subjective opinions to circumvent Scripture's plain, literal, historical, and grammatical interpretation. Ironically, the person willing to interpret or reinterpret a Biblical text because of his commitment to a particular subjective ideology is often the same person who will proclaim that this type of textual manipulation represents eisegesis rather than exegesis.

Eisegesis is the attempt to make Bible verses say what I want them to say, regardless of their plain, literal, historical and grammatical context and meaning. Scriptures that present a possible conflict with my beliefs get ignored or redefined to agree with my position. Cultists are guilty of practicing eisegesis. As Christians we can and should do a better job of handling Scripture than they do.

What exactly was Jesus saying in Matthew 16:22–23 when he referred to Peter as Satan?

> *And Peter took Him aside and began to rebuke Him,*
> *saying, "God forbid it, Lord! This shall never*
> *happen to You." But He turned and said to Peter,*
> *"Get behind Me, Satan! You are a stumbling block*
> *to Me; for you are not setting your mind on God's*
> *interests, but man's."*

What does Jesus mean by this comment? Nobody knows for certain although it is clear that Jesus is declaring that someone or something other than the Spirit of God is controlling Peter's thinking. At that moment, Jesus identified Peter as Satan. If this is the plain, literal, historical and grammatical reading of this verse, what are its implications in relation to the question of whether or not a demon has the potential ability to control the thinking of someone who sincerely loves God? It is interesting, once again, to note that a believer's battle centers in his mind.

There is only one name given under heaven whereby a person can be saved. (Acts 4:12) That name is Jesus Christ. There is only one foundation for eternal salvation. That foundation is Jesus Christ. (1 Corinthians 3:11) If you belong to Jesus Christ, your salvation has been signed in blood, purchased at a great price and sealed by the Holy Spirit (Ephesians 1:11–14; 1 Peter 1:17–21), guaranteeing that you are heaven bound. Will Scripture support just as clearly the teaching that Satan cannot occupy, control or demonize a true believer? No, it will not. If a person still chooses to argue that we cannot use Scripture to prove the demonization of a believer, it is certainly honest and accurate to acknowledge that Scripture, at the very least, allows for this possibility. We also must agree that many equally dedicated and educated pastors and teachers agree to disagree on this subject. It would be just as accurate to say that you can't use Scripture to prove a Christian cannot be demonized as to say that you cannot prove that Christians can be demonized. The burden of proof has nothing to do with traditions or denominational positions, which ultimately represent nothing more than manmade constructs to supposedly point us back to Scripture. Our position on spiritual warfare must be consistent with Scripture and able to pass a reality test as we deal with people for whom Christ died. Real needs of real people should take precedent over theological speculations and private agendas.

If Scripture allows the possibility of the demonization of Christians, and if mature and trusted Christian laymen, leaders and missionaries share a common testimony about the validity of this experience, then what are the motivations and insights of those who deny these collective testimonies other than personal opinions? Christians are welcome to challenge various theological perspectives and even to write position papers on their viewpoints. But within the context discussed in this book, a person's view on the subject of spiritual warfare should not be a Christian litmus test for theological orthodoxy any more than whether a person is covenant or dispensational in theological persuasion. Jesus will no doubt settle some disagreements when we see Him face to face, but until that time comes, the fact is that on some positions, solid, Evangelical, fundamental, Bible-believing, born-again Christians hold competing positions. Equally sincere Christians disagree on the timing of the return of Christ. Someone is going to be surprised. People who challenge the theological orthodoxy of Christian luminaries like John MacArthur or Charles Swindoll because these men do not completely agree on various points about spiritual warfare should be ashamed. Differing views on the deity of Jesus Christ and the inspiration of Scripture can, and often do, provide dividing lines that determine Christian orthodoxy. Differing views on other topics, including spiritual warfare in general and the demonization of believers specifically, do not and should not represent this same type of litmus test used for determining theological orthodoxy.

If a person suspects he is demonized, must he have someone else pray with him to make the demons leave or can he take care of it by himself? Does successful deliverance ministry demand a special gift from God?

A person does not need to pray with someone else to make demons leave. Demons respond to believers because of their authority as members of the body of Christ, not because of their gifts, talents or personality. Deliverance ministry doesn't depend upon any particular personality type or spiritual gift. My authority is no different than any other Christian's delegated authority. Jesus Christ delegates my authority and victory over demons. A person would be hard pressed to argue that the twelve (Matthew 10), much less the seventy (Luke 10), all had the same spiritual gifts. Clearly they did not all have the same spiritual gifts or personality types, but they all had the same delegated authority over demonic spirits. Each true believer receives spiritual gifts to exercise in service for the common good of the body of Christ (1 Corinthians 12:7, 1 Peter 4:10–11). Paul argues with force in 1 Corinthians 12 that believers do not all have the same gifts. In Christ there is purposed diversity (1 Corinthians 12:4–11, 28–31). We need each other's particular contributions for the body of Christ to build itself up in love with efficiency and effectiveness (Ephesians 4:11–16). Each of us has a divinely ordained and necessary place in God's supernatural service (John 15:16; Ephesians 2:10).

Delegated authority though is something He gave each of us when He placed us into the body of Christ and seated us with Him in the heavenlies far above all rule, authority, power, and dominion (Ephesians 1:20–2:7). The payment made for each of us was the same, and the resources available to us are the same. The New Testament nowhere teaches that the particular spiritual gifts God has given us limit the delegated authority and divine power we have received. In Christ there is supposed to be unity in diversity (1Corinthians 12:12–13, 20–27 Ephesians 4:1–6, 4:16). We have different jobs by divine design, but we are equal in value and delegated authority because of our relationship to Jesus Christ. Red, yellow, black, and white, we are all equally precious in His sight. Isn't that the essential message of Galatians 3:28?

> *There is neither Jew nor Greek, there is neither*
> *slave nor free man, there is neither male nor*
> *female; for you are all one in Christ Jesus.*

The report brought back to the Savior in Luke 10 was that *even demons are subject to us in Your name.* The key to the authority this diversely gifted group of men experienced over demons had nothing to do with their own authority or abilities. Their victory had everything to do with their position in Christ and the authority He delegated to them. The world, the flesh and the devil are as active today as they were in the first century. Names and faces have changed, but our opposition has not, nor has our position in Christ.

Christians who assume our authority has changed in this battle, even though the evil we face is still the same, argue from silence and theological presuppositions they cannot support Biblically. It simply does not make sense that God would command that we contend for the faith once for all delivered to the saints (Jude 3) and then withdraw the authority and power He has given us to carry on the fight with success.

Demons do not respect or fear Christians involved in deliverance ministries. They fear Christ who lives in all true believers, and they respond to the authority He has delegated to His ambassadors. Our authority is higher than their authority because our Master is greater than their master. Christ defeated Satan through His death, burial and resurrection. Demons understand this, even if they try to play dumb or become belligerent when challenged.

The key elements to deliverance are: 1) the volitional decision to consciously surrender every area of our lives to the control of Christ, 2) <u>confession</u> of all known sins, 3) the <u>canceling</u> of all footholds or ground being held against the demonized person, 4) identifying spirits and <u>commanding</u> them to leave, and 5) good follow-up.

I have been told that the authority Christ delegated to believers over demonic powers was limited to the original apostles. That aspect of ministry stopped with the death of the last apostle.

Luke 10:17–20 and Luke 9:49–50 clearly argue against the idea that exercising authority over demons was limited to the original twelve apostles.

> *And the **seventy** returned with joy, saying, "Lord, even the demons are subject to us in Your name." And He said to them, "I was watching Satan fall from heaven like lightning. Behold, I have given you authority to tread upon serpents and scorpions, and over all the power of the enemy, and nothing shall injure you. Nevertheless do not rejoice in this, that the spirits are subject to you, but rejoice that your names are recorded in heaven."*   Luke 10:17–20

> *And John answered and said, "Master, we saw someone casting out demons in Your name; and we tried to hinder him because he does not follow along with us." But Jesus said to him, "Do not hinder him; for he who is not against you is for you."* Luke 9:49–50

These passages indicate with unequivocal clarity that the Jesus did not limit the authority to help demonized individuals to just the original apostles. They also make it clear that it did not surprise or bother Jesus that men outside of His original twelve disciples were confronting demons in His name. When John the Apostle informed Jesus of this occurrence, Jesus did not rebuke the individual confronting demons in His name. Instead, He told His disciples not to hinder those actively involved in deliverance ministry. This is hardly the response you would expect from Jesus if He had limited His delegated authority over demons to just His twelve disciples.

Jesus understood His authority over the devil and his host, and they understood and acknowledged His authority, too. It is obvious to the unbiased reader that Jesus delegated authority over demons to His original disciples and taught them how to confront demonic spirits with effectiveness. But it is just as clear that the seventy shared in the benefits of the same lessons because they exercised the same delegated authority.

Matthew 28:18–20 and John 17:7–23 both indicate that Jesus commanded the Apostles to make disciples and instructed them to teach others the things He had first taught them.

> *And Jesus came up and spoke to them, saying, "All authority has been given to Me in heaven and on earth. "Go therefore and make disciples of all the nations, baptizing them in the name of the Father and the Son and the Holy Spirit, teaching them to observe all that I commanded you; and lo, I am with you always, even to the end of the age."* Matthew 28:18–20

> *"Now they have come to know that everything You have given Me is from You; for the words which You gave Me I have given to them; and they received them and truly understood that I came forth from You, and they believed that You sent Me.*

> *"I ask on their behalf; I do not ask on behalf of the world, but of those whom You have given Me; for they are Yours; and all things that are Mine are Yours, and Yours are Mine; and I have been glorified in them.*

> *"I am no longer in the world; and yet they themselves are in the world, and I come to You Holy Father, keep them in Your name, the name which You have given Me, that they may be one even as We are.*

"While I was with them, I was keeping them in Your name which You have given Me; and I guarded them and not one of them perished but the son of perdition, so that the Scripture would be fulfilled.

"But now I come to You; and these things I speak in the world so that they may have My joy made full in themselves.

"I have given them Your word; and the world has hated them, because they are not of the world, even as I am not of the world.

"I do not ask You to take them out of the world, but to keep them from the evil one.

"They are not of the world, even as I am not of the world.

"Sanctify them in the truth; Your word is truth.

"As You sent Me into the world, I also have sent them into the world.

"For their sakes I sanctify Myself, that they themselves also may be sanctified in truth.

"I do not ask on behalf of these alone, but for those also who believe in Me through their word; that they may all be one; even as You, Father, are in Me and I in You, that they also may be in Us, so that the world may believe that You sent Me.

"The glory which You have given Me I have given to them, that they may be one, just as We are one;

I in them and You in Me, that they may be perfected in unity, so that the world may know that You sent Me, and loved them, even as You have loved Me.
John 17:7–23

Are we to assume that the teaching lessons the Apostles shared with the disciples they trained did not include instruction on spiritual warfare and demonic confrontation? Why? Paul told

Timothy to entrust the things he had shared with him to faithful men who were to repeat the same process with others.

> *The things which you have heard from me in the*
> *presence of many witnesses, entrust these to faithful*
> *men who will be able to teach others also.* 2
> Timothy 2:2

Are we to assume that Paul failed to teach Timothy anything about spiritual warfare and demonization? Why would he have done this? Where and when did Jesus or Paul ever declare in the New Testament that a Christian's ability to confront demons was a special gift or ability that would pass away with the death of the last Apostle? Those verses do not exist. To argue that Jesus and Paul did communicate that message with their disciples, but that the New Testament just didn't record those particular conversations, is an argument from silence that is deplorable and unconvincing.

I have heard speakers say that if Christians working with demonized individuals was such an important part of the disciples' training, why didn't Jesus, Paul or at least one of the other New Testament writers include a chapter or a book on the topic? The argument is that since there is not a chapter or a book dedicated to this topic that it is of no real consequence or importance. I have already responded to this question, but it should suffice to say that if we held the topic of the Trinity to the same standard, none of us would believe or teach that God is triune in nature and one in essence. If teaching truth is the goal and helping others the job, it's time to agree to drop the double standard held by many sincere Christians when addressing the subject of demonization.

Arguments from silence can cut both ways. Apparently heaven was also a topic of little or no importance to Jesus or the New Testament writers because we can't find a single chapter or book dedicated to it. How about the cessation of all sign gifts or the pre-trib, mid-trib, post-trib or no-trib return of Jesus? Do you have the final word on whether or not God has divided time and His economy through covenants or dispensations? Does our position on the subject of covenant or dispensational theology really represent a litmus test for orthodoxy? If so, who is the one on this side of heaven that is going to determine the difference in the sincerity and godliness of Charles Swindoll, David Jeremiah, Charles Colson or R. C. Sproul?

How many chapters or books does the New Testament dedicate to a clear articulation of these topics or theological positions? Apparently they were just not that important to Jesus or the New Testament writers if we follow the same logic applied to the topic of spiritual warfare and confronting demonic spirits. There are some subjects that equally sincere Christians have agreed to disagree about and to wait for Jesus Christ to settle when we are all bowing before Him. When the Scripture is clear, we must have the courage to speak clearly. When Scripture is ambiguous or less than clear, at least within our current understanding, we must have the maturity to extend the same grace to others that we want extended to us. To do less is not only hypocritical, it is arrogant.

To assume that the authority Christ delegated to His disciples over demons suddenly stopped with the death of the last apostle is a case that some Christians try to make in spite of their tortured use of Scripture and arguments from silence. We should recognize that besides this position's painful inconsistency, its adherents typically support it by conjecture, inference and opinion rather than Scripture. That's because Scripture nowhere demands that conclusion.

What exactly does the term "ground" mean in relation to Christians and demonization?

Ground is another term used for permission to control a place, a space or a territory in a Christian's life. According to Ephesians 4:27, unconfessed sins potentially provide the devil and his demons with a handhold or a foothold of opportunity (*topos*) to exploit a Christian. This allows them to actively attack a Christian in a manner beyond simple oppression. These handholds or footholds represent chinks in our armor. Even good armor will bend and eventually break if hit in the same spot often enough. When we fail to confess our sin, demons regard this action as giving them ground or permission to attack us through that soft spot. It is as though they're saying something like this:

> *You know you're supposed to walk with God, but*
> *you're refusing to do things His way. If you don't*
> *want to do things His way, then you are by*
> *definition agreeing to do things our way. There are*
> *no other choices. You are either for Christ or you*
> *are against Him. If you fail to stand with Jesus on a*
> *particular issue, then by choice or default you have*
> *sided with us on the matter. We now hold this as*
> *ground or permission to attack you until you submit*
> *that specific area of your life to Jesus Christ and the*
> *control of the Holy Spirit.*

How do demons invade or demonize a true Christian?

There is one primary route for the demonization of Christians and one secondary route. The most common way Christians become demonized is through the consequences of handholds and footholds mentioned in Ephesians 4:27, which are the results of unconfessed sins. Habitual sin will allow a small crack to become a crater in our armor. Given enough time a small handhold or foothold can become a crack crater or ledge large enough to put your hand in or your foot upon. A solid ledge can eventually turn into an ice cave large enough to throw in a sleeping bag. As days become weeks and weeks turn into months, a cave can become a temporary home.

The second way believers give demons ground and access is through ancestral or generational sins. The New Testament nowhere abrogates the Biblical revelation in the Old Testament that sins of adults can pass to their children. When parents sin, they are hurting not only themselves, they are also potentially setting their children up for demonic bondage. The thoughts of our sins held against our children should work as a deterrent against planned sin and as a motivator to strive for godliness.

Unfortunately, a growing number of parents view children as personal liabilities rather than gifts from God. It shouldn't be a surprise that the numbers of individuals I work with who have problems with ancestral sins are steadily growing.

What is the difference between attacks of "oppression" that all Christians experience at one time or another, and "demonization" that all Christians do not experience?

Oppression is always external in nature whereas demonization is something different and far more severe in nature. Christians struggling with demonic oppression experience seasons of relief. The battles of demonized Christians are daily and often feel like they never let up for more than a very short period of time. A demon might briefly lay low as a strategic counter attack. But remember, they do not go on extended vacations or take sabbatical breaks from their work. The intensity level of attack is far greater for a demonized Christian than it is for a person having to extinguish an occasional flaming missile. It is very difficult for a Christian who has only experienced oppression to understand the intensity of the attack demonized Christians endure on a daily basis. This may also help explain why two Christians with similar backgrounds before receiving Jesus Christ as their Lord and Savior can have such contrasting responses afterwards. One person hits the ground with his spiritual life running full throttle and never looks back, while the other, although just as sincere in his original commitment to Christ, has an overwhelming battle and an unrelenting sense of condemnation and unworthiness.

It's possible that one is simply more committed to Christ and to studying and applying God's Word to his life than the other. Lazy, compromised Christians who always have an excuse for their sin fill this world. Maybe one person has a genetic predisposition to an addiction and the other does not. I suppose either alternative is possible, but there is a third option.

Have you ever considered the possibility that one of these believers had been demonized and the other had not? The mental anguish of demonic accusation can be debilitating, discouraging and emotionally draining. The first person recognizes the mental proposition to step back into sin as a passing arrow, a demonic lie, and rejects it in much the same way Jesus responded to the devil's solicitations to sin in Matthew 4. However, the second individual, although he doesn't lack sincerity of faith, may face a constant barrage of arrows and demonic accusations that he battles 24/7 with little or no relief, regardless of how often he prays or reads his Bible. At some point, such people throw up their hands and say, "I guess I must not be a good Christian, and it's never going to change, so why continue to fight it?"

The first person looks at the second wondering, *So what's the big problem? Pray about it and move on*! Meanwhile, the second individual is looking at the first and thinking to himself, *Why is everything so easy for him and a constant struggle for me? I guess God either doesn't love me as much as He loves him or I really am the failure I keep hearing about in my mind.*

Demons are neither omnipotent nor omniscient. They can't bother every Christian at the same time or with similar severity, nor can they take advantage of every sinning believer. The reality is that there are just not that many of them to go around. In addition, some Christians have actually learned to resist them in the delegated authority of the Lord Jesus Christ. Other Christians run from them in fear, which simply invites more attacks. Is it possible that some Christians already experienced demonic bondage before their conversions or have given ground to demonic spirits after their salvation, where other Christians have never given ground to demons before or after their conversion? Although both responded to the good news of the gospel by grace through faith, one lives his new life in Christ with joy while the other endures his salvation as a job. He lives with constant feelings of failure, guilt, false guilt and unworthiness.

The job of an oppressing demon is to solicit the believer to sin. The job of a demon that has invaded, infested or demonized a Christian is to destroy that person. Some Christians assume they can turn godliness on and off. Weekends and vacation are a time to relax from spiritual commitments. Demons don't go on vacations or take recreational breaks from their destructive work, though they may lay low for a while to avoid exposure. Their time is short, and they know it. They are committed to taking as many captives with them as possible. Their attitude seems to be: *If I'm going down, you're going with me*.

It is unfortunate that so many Christians do not approach their work of service sharing the message of new life in Christ with as much dedication and energy as demons do their message of death. Demonization rather than godliness may also explain, in part, the seemingly tireless energy of those who preach another gospel than the one that was delivered once, for all time, to the saints (Jude 3).

Is deliverance ministry really as chaotic and vulgar as the movie industry portrays it?

The movie industry gives more credit to the devil and his demons than it does to the Lord Jesus Christ. As I mentioned earlier, when I am involved in warfare counseling at the office the other pastors on staff and our secretaries are not typically aware of whether I am doing warfare counseling, marriage counseling, discipleship or sharing the gospel. If a person working in deliverance ministry is allowing screaming and overly dramatic sensationalism to occur, he is either unaware he can prevent the circus atmosphere or he is deliberately allowing it to happen.

Do you aggressively pursue individuals you believe are struggling with demons?

I usually will not pursue people regarding demons and deliverance, even if I feel certain that is the nature of their struggle. Why? The demonized individual's will, his willingness to stand in faith rather than to run in fear, and his complete honesty in addressing sin are more important than who is guiding his time confronting demons. A demonized individual's resolute persistence to stand on God's promises is even more important than my resolution to stand with him in his fight. If he has agreed to talk with me for any reason other than the fact that he wants to walk with God and is willing to put anything and everything between himself and God on the table through confession, the demons will refuse to leave because they will still hold ground through unconfessed and uncanceled sin. I have learned the long and hard way that it's better to pray and wait for people who want help rather than aggressively pursue individuals inconvenienced by the results of their sin but unwilling to turn their backs on it.

Why are so many Christians either afraid or unwilling to confront the subject of spiritual warfare in general and the subject of demonization in particular?

There is probably not a one size fits all answer to this question. However, after working in this area of ministry for many years, I am willing to take an honest swing at the answer.

First, most Christian circles outside of charismatic-oriented churches and groups typically ignore the areas of spiritual warfare and demonization. Many non-charismatic Christians are not only fearful of a teaching that their churches have largely ignored, they are also afraid that other Christians will ridicule, vilify and socially stigmatize them if they get involved with demons or openly associate with people willing to do so.

Second, to be fair to some of our fearful non-charismatic brethren, some circles have used and abused this subject. This at least partially explains some Christians' hesitation or resistance. They fear identification with those individuals or groups who allow this ministry to turn into an infomercial or a chaotic circus to draw viewers or raise revenues for their particular ministries. Blaming demons for everything in some circles has promoted an attitude of rejecting anyone and anything remotely associated with demons in other circles. Promoting the positions of either side of this swinging pendulum as normative for everyone is not helpful.

Third, too many Christians care more about their peers viewing them as politically correct rather than Biblically correct. The popular media have consistently promoted the ridicule of God, Satan and demons in a fashion that makes Christians look dumber than the common ancestor of the apes we supposedly evolved from according to materialistic naturalists. In other cases, these ideological humanists so aggrandize and glorify Satan that some Christians fear even discussing the subject. Christians who fear a backlash from the media or their neighbors and colleagues seem to work harder at blending into society than opposing its accelerating slide into godlessness. They too often spend more time accommodating the lies of naturalism, relativism, Darwinism and Marxism than they do promoting the deity of the Lord Jesus Christ and the inerrancy of Scripture. God calls Christians to walk in the light and expose evil, not excuse it, i.e. Matthew 5:12–16, Colossians 2:8, Titus1:9 and Jude 3.

Fourth, some Christians give Satan and his demons too much credit. Whether the problem is ignorance, superstition or arrogance, many Christians are more fearful of the problems demons may try to inflict upon them than they are confident that their Savior is able and willing to protect them against demonic attack.

Demons are intelligent, supernatural opponents who are intent upon destroying Christians and humiliating Jesus Christ by any means possible. But they are not equals, and we should never treat them as such. God commands Christians to resist demons, not run from them. When Christians confront a demonized person, they need to do so from a position of strength as victors rather than cowering in fear as helpless victims. Paul understood this when he told the believers in Rome that if God is for us it doesn't matter who is against us (Romans 8:31). Luke, Paul's traveling partner, physician and disciple, understood this when he stated in Luke 10:18 that we have received authority to step on demons. The Apostle John understood this same truth when he declared that the One who is for us is greater than the one who is against us (1 John 4:4).

When Christians show fear before a demon or treat it as an equal, this emboldens it to pursue the attack. It rightly surmises that a fearful believer has more concern about a defeated enemy than a risen Savior. This is an insult to our risen Savior, the Lord Jesus Christ. I have witnessed many demons who declared that their ground for tormenting a Christian was the fact that the Christian feared them and was willing to listen to or entertain their lies. Attempting to pacify bullies, like terrorists, usually just enables them to continue their reign of terror.

10

Demonic Warfare:

Subtleties in the Battle

The most common response I hear from demonized Christians is that they undergo a constant mental bombardment of godless accusation. No matter what they do, it's wrong. No matter how sincere they are about attempting to walk with Jesus, they aren't sincere enough. If they pray, it's incomplete. If they read their Bibles, they're too stupid to understand what it means and lack the discipline to obey it anyway, so why try. There is always something left undone, leaving a constant sense of guilt, condemnation and failure.

When demons feel emboldened, it is not unusual for them to attack a person's subconscious in an attempt to disrupt their sleep. The growing fatigue and mental confusion associated with sleep deprivation can eventually wear down and discourage even a strong soldier. Christians harassed by demonic spirits, particularly at night, consistently describe a sense of something in the room that they may or may not see and a feeling of total paralysis. Their minds are fully functioning, but their bodies seem unable to respond. They want to turn on a light, but they can't move their arms. They want to pray out loud, but nothing comes out of their mouths. The sensations of hot pressure pushing down on their chests and of the hair on their bodies standing up are also common.

The realities of demonic attack are as different as the particular people and demons involved, but several things often seem predictable and consistent. If demons hold ground against an individual, they will seldom volunteer to cooperate or leave. There is often a correlation between a demon's stubborn arrogance and the security or authority it assumes it holds regarding the individual it has demonized. When demons understand that the struggling person has decided to resist by removing the ground and standing on his positional authority in Christ, the battle is short and to the point. The good guys win and the bad guys lose—every time. When demons still hold ground because of some unconfessed sin and know that the person they are troubling is unwilling to freely and completely submit his entire life to Christ's lordship, the battle can become arduous, confusing, frustrating and drawn out. Demons do not seem to have to freely cooperate in the process of deliverance when the persons they are attacking don't care about actively resisting their attacks.

A person who receives Jesus as Savior but habitually ignores Him as Lord is potentially setting himself up for a walk with Christ that more closely resembles a job to endure than new life in Christ to enjoy. Picking and choosing which sins to confess or ignore may work if pleasing man is the goal. But we should understand that Christians who refuse to confront habitual sin in their lives are handing out an open invitation for demonic bondage, whether they realize they are or not.

Working with demonized Christians over the last twenty-five years has taught me several bottom lines regarding spiritual warfare with demonic spirits. We are on the side of the One who has ultimately won this conflict and should walk worthy of our calling in the Lord Jesus Christ. First John 4:4 is a reminder that the One who is in us is greater than the one who is against us. This should be a comfort and a confidence. When a born-again Christian is one hundred percent honest regarding his sin and willingly puts everything on the table that he is aware of between himself and God by confessing and canceling sin, he will win this spiritual battle.

On the other hand, when a true follower of the Lord Jesus Christ chooses to hide, ignore or run from sin that has opened ground to demonic spirits he may suffer ongoing mental, emotional and sometimes even physical torment. This is true regardless of the person's position in Christ, even though that believer is still heaven bound according to 1 Corinthians 3:15.

Demons are neither all powerful nor everywhere present. But they understand their work better than we do, they have had more practice perfecting their battle plans, and they are tenacious in their efforts to destroy the lives and testimonies of born-again Christians. Victory belongs to believers positionally because of their relationship with Christ. But playing with sin or excusing it isn't resisting demonic attack, it's inviting it. James and Peter are both clear that victory over the devil will occur when we resist the devil in humble obedience to God (James 4:7–10; 1 Peter 5:6–9). But playing with sin is to a demon what blood in the water is to a shark.

Committed Christians who mean business don't have a difficult time getting free from demonic bondage. Christians ready to confront demonic bondage are willing to confess any and all sin they are aware of that stands between themselves and God—no hiding, no excuses, no exceptions. They are also willing to submit themselves and every area of their lives under the control of the Holy Spirit and the lordship of the Lord Jesus Christ. Galatians 2:20 is a positional truth and growing life experience, not just a verse to quote or to debate. Christians may feel physically trapped, emotionally traumatized, mentally tortured, angry, helpless, depressed, defeated or embarrassed by the effects of demonic strongholds. But if they are also unwilling to confess the sin(s) that opened the door to demonic bondage in the first place or are too afraid to confront the demonic archers mentally accusing them, they will have a far more difficult time. *Play the game, pay the dues* is a truism regarding spiritual warfare that we cannot cheat regardless of the rationalization for ignoring, ridiculing or rejecting the realities of this debilitating spiritual battle.

There is another subtle ploy I have observed on several occasions. Sometimes when demonized Christians have scheduled an appointment to confront demonic accusers, they will cancel at the last minute. They tell me that something has just come up and they will have to reschedule. They feel suddenly sick, their kids are now sick or fighting, their car won't start, the boss called them in unexpectedly to work different hours, they suddenly feel at peace and assume there is no need to keep the appointment and so forth. The issues delaying the appointment aren't necessarily bad; they just keep the meeting from taking place. I have had individuals literally get sick at my office door as they were preparing to walk in. I have had people tell me that they have to use the bathroom over and over, suspiciously timed, just as we are ready to confront demons. I have watched alert people fall asleep right in front of me in a moment. On other occasions people in the midst of demonic confrontation have said, "I just can't hear what you're saying" even though we are only a few feet apart and speaking directly to each other.

It is also not unusual for the appointee to say that he's afraid to come in because demons have terrorized him mentally all day or he has had nightmares the night before. An all-too-familiar voice told him that his loved ones will meet harm if he follows through with the appointment to explore or confront this issue. Others have told me that they couldn't get the thought out of their minds that it will ruin them socially if word gets out regarding talking with a pastor about demons. Still others have told me that they wanted to cancel their appointments because they feared they would just be wasting my time.

Bargaining can also appear as part of a predictable pattern of mentally bombarding an individual determined to get help against demons. What do the demons promise? Whatever the propositioned person is willing to buy seems fair game. Money, women, men, financial raises, drugs, popularity, power and super spirituality are all familiar offerings.

The excuses or rationalizations are different, but the results in each case are the same. Whatever you do, "don't go through with the appointment or attempt to get help."

> *You'll never get us all, and we'll be back. You're going to look like a fool. No rational human being hears voices or goes to church for help. You're making all of this up for attention; just ignore it and it will go away. You need to talk to a real counselor to get help, not a preacher. He probably doesn't know what he's doing anyway. Things will get worse if you make us go. We will get your loved ones if you attempt to make us leave. We will get you money, women, men, if you will let us stay. Everything is better, don't bother the pastor, there are other people who need his attention more than you. Call him later if things get worse.*

The list goes on, but the bottom line is clear. Don't confront this issue or else.

Demons aren't stupid. If they need to intimidate someone to keep him from getting help, they will become master intimidators. If they need to just lay low for a few hours or days to avoid conflict and avoid exposure, they will gladly lighten up for a short period of time. If they must play the pity card, they can do that also.

> *Hell is a terrible place. A real Christian wouldn't condemn anyone to go there. Christians are commanded to love their enemies and their neighbors as themselves. Christians are supposed to have the courage to bear their cross without taking revenge. We're just doing our jobs. A real Christian would show compassion and pity.*

Confusion is another favorite trick demons like to play, especially if the person guiding the session is inexperienced or the demonized individual is particularly fearful or skeptical. If successful they may stall the session before it ever gets off the ground by overloading the troubled person with conflicting information and doubt.

When confession has occurred and ground(s) canceled, answers are usually simple and straightforward. Following is an example of how demons no longer holding ground might answer questions put to them in the name and authority of the Lord Jesus Christ.

In the name of the Lord Jesus Christ, what is your name?

(Death.)

In the name of the Lord Jesus Christ, what work have you been commissioned to do?

 (Destroy her. Kill her. We are going to destroy her.)

In the name of the Lord Jesus Christ, by what means do you hope to accomplish this work?

(Fear, drugs, self-destruction, deception, sex. Nobody likes her.)

In the name of the Lord Jesus Christ, what lies have you been telling (Spungetta) on a habitual basis?

(We tell her that she's not really a Christian and that God doesn't love her any more. We tell her that she has committed the unforgivable sin and will never be forgiven. We tell her that nobody loves her, not her family, her pastor or friends. She doesn't have any real friends because she's sick and nobody wants to be around her. She's damaged goods, nobody likes her. We tell her that she's stupid and that there's no reason to read the Bible because she won't understand it anyway. We tell her no one will ever believe her testimony because they know she will eventually fall back into sin again. We tell her she cannot live without drugs and sex. She cannot escape her fate.)

In the name of the Lord Jesus Christ, do you hold any ground that keeps you from leaving (Spungetta) upon command?

(No.)

You understand that you are going to leave (Spungetta) upon command and take all of your works and effects with you along with all of your associates and their works and effects too?

(Yes. Just get it over with.)

Demons who still hold ground and want to disrupt a session through mental confusion, intimidation and/or fear might respond to these same questions in this manner.

In the name of the Lord Jesus Christ, what is your name?

(Legion, Death…you figure it out. You're making this up. You just read the name Legion in the Bible. No demon is named Death. You're making this up and look really stupid. Get out of here with some dignity while you still can.)

In the name of the Lord Jesus Christ, is your name Legion or Death?

(Maybe, maybe. Yes, no, yes, no. By what authority do you ask? We run the world. You don't know what you're doing.)

In the name of the Lord Jesus Christ, what work have you been commissioned to do against (Spungetta)?

(We won't tell you, and you won't figure it out. You're making all of this up.)

In the name of the Lord Jesus Christ, by what means do you hope to accomplish your work?

(We love her. We're trying to help her. It's you Christians who are hurting people. If you would quit bothering her she could live a normal life.)

In the name of the Lord Jesus Christ, what lies have you been telling (Spungetta) on a habitual basis?

(She doesn't know truth from error. She can't think straight anymore. She is losing her mind. She is a fake. You are a fake. This is a fake. This isn't going to work. This is too confusing. She is too tired. God does not love her anymore. You don't know what you are doing. This is all in her mind. Run. Get out of here. Nobody in this church cares about her. Kill yourself, there is no hope.)

In the name of the Lord Jesus Christ, do you hold any ground that keeps you from leaving (Spungetta) upon command?

(Yes/no, yes/no. You won't figure it out. We'll never leave.)

Remember that demons have several advantages over Christians in the arena of spiritual warfare. For instance: 1) Many Christians are afraid to exercise their delegated authority over spirits. 2) Demons have been on the job longer than the Christian. They exploit both of these advantages in a cruel fashion. They have had far more time learning how to perfect their skills and schemes than we have had time to learn how to recognize or respond to them. God's children get no second chances on life (Hebrews 9:27), but many demons have stealthily cycled through assignments generation after generation, largely unrecognized and unchallenged.

We are at a distinct disadvantage in these infernal battles unless we resolutely stand on our faith in Christ and our delegated authority over all the powers of the enemy, and unless we know the Word of God. Who has the advantage in the fight when Christians are afraid to even read about spiritual warfare, much less engage enemies? An inferior army, well organized and committed to a common cause, will beat a superior army that is asleep on the job. God's children sacrifice victories they should win because of fear, pride, apathy, ignorance, misunderstanding and lack of perseverance and determination.

The Apostle Paul told the Corinthians that they were not ignorant of the purposes (methodologies) of the devil (2 Corinthians 2:11). He could not and would not make the same claim for most Christians living in North America in the twenty-first century. Christians, by and large, ignore or shy away from spiritual warfare. Pantheists and New Agers embrace demonic spirits as ascended masters or spirit guides, and spiritists often celebrate contact with demonic spirits as some sort of spiritual enlightenment.

As Christians we are too often ignorant of both our enemy and our available resources, and too fearful or proud to admit it. Through Christ we are more than conquerors. But apart from Him we can do absolutely nothing in this battle. It is important to understand and remember that spiritual warfare is primarily mental. Second Corinthians 11:1–4 says:

> *I wish that you would bear with me in a little foolishness; but indeed you are bearing with me. For I am jealous for you with a godly jealousy; for I betrothed you to one husband, that to Christ I might present you as a pure virgin. But I am afraid, lest as the serpent deceived Eve by his craftiness, your minds should be led astray from the simplicity and purity of devotion to Christ. For if one comes and preaches another Jesus, who we have not preached, or you receive a different spirit which you have not received, or a different gospel which you have not accepted, you bear this beautifully.*

Eve was deceived. Her initial battle was mental. She entertained and lost a dialogue with Satan before she decided to eat the fruit. For whatever reason, when we surrender the mental battle in supernatural conflict, we are encouraging and promoting our own defeat. It's one thing to lose a battle because we were outsmarted. It's another thing to lose by self-imposed ignorance. *Win in your mind and you will win in your life. Lose in your mind and it is just a matter of time before you will be losing in your life. We eventually end up acting upon those things we rationalize in our minds*. The bottom line is that when we choose to lose battles in our mind with the world, the flesh or the devil, it's just a matter of time before we will lose those battles in life.

My experience through years of dealing with oppressed or demonized Christians is that the battle is often one-sided because believers seldom recognize the true nature of their struggle nor do they understand how they should respond when they do become suspicious of demonic activity. It is one thing for a Christian to leave a person languishing in mental and emotional pain because he is unable to help that person. It's another thing, however, to leave a person in agonizing mental paralysis because we are uncomfortable or unwilling to reach out to those in need. We may react this way because we selfishly fear for our own safety. Or worse, perhaps we are more concerned about what others will think of us than the brother or sister who is suffering in silent torment. We need more good Samaritans and less religious Pharisees.

Examples of the battle

How subtle can the battle get helping Christians confront demons? Let's look at some examples.

Eddie

Eddie was a very likable young person who was popular with his peers. His home life was complicated for a variety of reasons. Eddie happened to be adopted. He often told others that his parents treated their biological children with favoritism over him. He didn't like himself and was tired of feeling like he could never measure up to others' expectations. By the time he was a senior in high school he had already tried to kill himself several times. His family called me at 1:20 a.m. after his latest attempt to kill himself. Eddie had hung himself in his garage. His brother or sister found him still alive, and his dad was able to get him down in time. His dad called me immediately and asked if I would come over right away.

I was surprised when I arrived to see Mr. Smith sprawled out on top of Eddie, desperately trying to hold him down. Eddie's dad had sweat dripping from his red face, and it was clear the twenty minutes it had taken me to get to the house had been a struggle. A betting person would have put his money on Mr. Smith because he was a large man, outweighing Eddie by at least a hundred pounds.

When I walked into the garage Mr. Smith said to me, "I can't hold on to him much longer."

I immediately said, "In the name of the Lord Jesus Christ release your control of the boy." Eddie instantly flattened out on the floor and went limp as his dad looked up in utter bewilderment.

I told Eddie to get up, to walk over to the family room and to sit on the couch. He walked there without saying a word. I quickly explained the concepts of ground rules, confessing sins and canceling grounds in relationship to demonization. I took nearly thirty minutes explaining to Eddie the importance of his will in this fight and the absolute necessity for his complete honesty in the confession and canceling of sins if he wanted freedom from demonic bondage. He said he understood and wanted to be free. He said he would do whatever it took to get things right with Christ so the demons would have to leave.

For several years Eddie had been struggling over his sexual orientation. He was experimenting with sexual immorality and clearly dominated by lust and sensuality. I assumed this was as obvious a point as any to begin the confrontation and demanded to know, in the name of the Lord Jesus Christ, if there was a demonic spirit in charge of this area of his life. Up to this time, Eddie had remained quiet and cooperative.

When I commanded any spirits working in the area of sexual immorality to come forward there was an immediate response. The demon in charge started saying, *"Eddie is ours and you cannot have him back. We love him more than Jesus does. We love him more than his family does. We won't let him go."* Eddie knew it was a lie that demons loved him more than Jesus Christ did, but he was scared. He had also grown accustomed to listening to this demon and his associates whisper lies to him.

I commanded the demon to describe the work it did and the lies it told Eddie on a regular basis. It admitted that the comment about loving Eddie more than Jesus was a lie. I asked the demon if it was responsible for making Eddie feel dirty, unforgivable and suicidal and for having sexually immoral thoughts after it planted those same thoughts in his mind in the first place. The demon laughed and said that was its job. It covered both sides of the coin in Eddie's life. First it tempted him to sin in his mind. Then once Eddie took the bait and responded in thought or action to the demon's suggestions, it told him he was committing sin that God would never forgive. It set him up and then knocked him down. It tempted Eddie and then condemned him for responding to its solicitation.

(It is important to remember that a demon's job is to tempt a person to express his or her sexuality outside of a Biblical definition of marriage between one man and one woman in the specific context of marriage. How this happens is not nearly as important to a demon as that it happens.)

I asked Eddie if he was ready to confess his sin and to ask God to cancel the ground he had given up so we could command the demon to leave. He said he was ready. We prayed together and then commanded the demon to leave. Usually the battle is over right there. God's side wins, the demons lose. But on this occasion the demon responded that it wouldn't leave and that it didn't have to go. I demanded to know what ground it still held to stay on. The demon said that Eddie didn't mean his prayer and that he didn't really want it to leave.

Demons do not have the power or authority to refuse to comply with a command in the name of the Lord Jesus Christ unless they still hold ground against the person they are tormenting. This response was unusual, so I asked Eddie what was going on. He was fully cognizant of the exchange.

Eddie had fooled his dad and me with his prayer. But he hadn't fooled the demon, and he certainly hadn't fooled God. He had hoped that he could say the right words, pray the prayer and the demon would leave. But he had no intention of changing his lifestyle. I asked Eddie if it was true what the demon said, that he did not mean his prayer and that he didn't want to turn his sexual desires over to God.

Eddie looked up at me and said, "I'm not sure I want to give up something I like for something I don't know whether I will like or not." At that point I told Eddie that the demons weren't going to leave unless he truly confessed his sin as sin and didn't excuse it. Parroting words about forgiveness that don't come from the heart is as useless in confronting demons as expecting salvation by praying a prayer that is not meant from the heart. Neither works.

Eddie was unwilling to submit this area of his life to the control of the Lord Jesus Christ. I told Eddie that if he ever decided he meant business and wanted to get things straightened out with God, I would be a phone call away. I went back home aching for Eddie and his family. To my knowledge, he never received help. Eddie's heart attitude toward his sin was more important than my potential participation in this process. Demons will leave when a Christian confesses the sin that has opened the door enabling their limited control and asks God to cancel the specific ground they hold. But they will not cooperate when Christians refuse to stand up and resist them.

The assumption that I have divine power and authority in spiritual warfare over demons because I have memorized a particular incantation, read a popular book or even attend a doctrinally sound church can be faulty. The sons of Sceva found this out in Paul's day (Acts 19:13–16). Right words and even sincere intentions do not necessarily come from a right relationship with God. Demons will leave when it is the only option left to them, but typically not until then. When confession of sin and canceling of ground occurs, demons will leave upon command. If an afflicted Christian's confession is insincere or he leaves ground uncanceled, demons will assume they still have permission to torment him.

Betty

Another example illustrating the subtlety of spiritual warfare involves a young woman named Betty. I received a message that a young lady had come to one of our daughter churches requesting help with a demonic issue. The pastor asked me sit in on the confrontation, and I agreed to. A retired career missionary, who was a friend and spiritual warfare mentor to me, was already talking to Betty when I arrived. As I walked into the church office I noticed a second young lady sitting on a couch apparently waiting to speak with someone.

The time with Betty was very frustrating. Although we confronted demons, they were arrogant and uncooperative. At the time I had worked very little in this area of ministry and was confused why the demons didn't leave immediately upon command and why answers to nearly every question seemed to be so painfully slow in coming and so arrogant in tone. My pastor/missionary/mentor friend finally told Betty to go home. She left and no one was rejoicing, except demons.

The next day I received another phone call from the same pastor at the same church requesting that I come over once again and talk with Betty. I was a little reluctant this time, but still agreed to do so. This time the results were very different. Demons responded immediately to questions and left quickly upon command. When Betty left, the retired missionary who had directed the session asked if I had noticed the difference between the responses she and the demons gave in this meeting and those they gave the day before. I told him the differences were so dramatically different that they were impossible to miss.

It seems that Betty had gone home after the confrontation the previous day and decided to begin reading her Bible. After reading most of the gospel of Matthew she decided she should not have to live the way she was living, called the church back and asked to come in for help. This time though she came alone, on her own volition and conviction, rather than being dragged in by her friend—the woman who had waited for her in the office the previous day.

Betty's confession of sin was genuine this time, and her request for God to cancel the subsequent grounds held against her was genuine, too. The demons quickly complied with the command for them to leave, and she walked out a free woman.

I learned a valuable lesson that day regarding a subtlety of spiritual warfare. Unless Christians are personally willing to resist the demons attacking them, and sincerely and genuinely confess and cancel all of the sin and ground held against them, the battle will not go well for them. The faith and resolute obedience of the person ensnared in demonic bondage is more important than the faith and sincerity of the one guiding that person through a deliverance process. I refuse to chase down people I think need to confront demons nor will I encourage others to do it. If you badger someone into confronting demons, how do you know whether that person truly wants help or is just trying to get you off his back?

Is it possible for men and women who love God dearly and who serve Him faithfully to struggle with demonic spirits in spiritual warfare for years and years? Yes, this is a real possibility. Demonic bondage is not a problem reserved just for neurotics, psychotics and insincere individuals claiming to be Christians but who bear no spiritual fruit. To the contrary, people who want to hear God's still small voice are often more susceptible to demonic deception than the proverbial bull in the china shop that refuses to take time to listen to God because he is so totally self-absorbed.

If demons cannot lead a Christian into obvious sins of the mind or flesh, they are more than willing to attempt to direct that person into battles with other Christians in areas that appear spiritual in nature. I suppose it makes Christians fighting and undermining other Christians seem more honorable because it appears to be a battle over something spiritual. Demons don't care what divides the body of Christ and compromises our personal or corporate testimony, only that we become consumed with infighting and have a testimony clouded with confusion rather than focused upon the Lord Jesus Christ. An example of this type of needless infighting is the way too many Christians handle the subject of spiritual gifts.

The Holy Spirit has given spiritual gifts to every true Christian. According to God's Word the determination of our gifting is left to His own choosing (1 Corinthians12:11, 18, 24, 28 and Hebrews 2:4). Demons love to move the joy and focus of a believer from God to man by redirecting our attention from the Giver of spiritual gifts to the gifts He has given. This type of deception is subtle because it appears so spiritual in nature. In reality, it too often divides believers into a non-Biblical caste system based upon our personal spiritual gifting. This sin also attacks our unity in Christ (Ephesians 4:1–6) and actually accuses God of favoritism based upon the perceived value of the gifts distributed.

Battles and divisions between churches or entire denominations regarding who is more spiritual based upon their spiritual gifting are disgraceful practices. They ultimately provide more aid to the enemies of Christ than assistance unifying and strengthening the body of Christ (1 Corinthians 12:25; 1 Corinthians 14:12). Our focus should be consistent obedience to God's commands (John 14:21–24).

> *...so that there may be no division in the body, but that the members may have the same care for one another.* 1 Corinthians 12:25

> *So also you, since you are zealous of spiritual gifts, seek to abound for the edification of the church.* 1 Corinthians 14:12

> *"He who has My commandments and keeps them is the one who loves Me; and he who loves Me will be loved by My Father, and I will love him and will disclose Myself to him."*

> *Judas (not Iscariot) said to Him, "Lord, what then has happened that You are going to disclose Yourself to us and not to the world?"*

Jesus answered and said to him, "If anyone loves Me, he will keep My word; and My Father will love him, and We will come to him and make Our abode with him.

"He who does not love Me does not keep My words; and the word which you hear is not Mine, but the Father's who sent Me. John 14:21–24

Sarah

Sarah came into my office and said she needed help. She explained that she didn't attend our church and that her husband was an elder in another church nearby. She had heard through the grapevine that I was comfortable working with Christians who were suffering from the debilitating discouragement and accusatory voices of demonic bondage and wanted to know if I would listen to her story.

I asked Sarah to clearly explain why she thought her struggles were demonic and not battles with the world, the flesh or her imagination. Unless the circumstances are unusual, my first appointment with an individual is usually to share how to experience consistent victory over the world and the flesh, and how to discern the difference between Holy Spirit conviction and demonic accusation. If problems are demonic, counsel on how to overcome the world and the flesh will not help. If, on the other hand, the problems go away by approaching them as conflicts with the world or the flesh, then there is no reason to blame demonic spirits for the problems.

Sarah's case was one of those unusual ones in which I felt comfortable confronting the demonic issue right away. She explained that several years earlier she had felt that somehow God was holding something back from her. She was convinced that she needed a second blessing of His grace for Him to prove His love for her and to provide her with a feeling of more power in her service for Him. She asked God for more of Jesus and confirmation by being able to speak in tongues, which her friends at church were encouraging her to do. Friends at her church told her that just accepting Jesus as Savior wasn't enough if she wanted to experience real power in her life and service. During a subsequent church service she said that she received the gift she had sought when the women placed their hands on her and prayed over her as she cried out, "Jesus, I want more—give me more."

Sarah told me that for several years it made her feel good when she exercised this gift, but that over the last year she was sensing some serious doubts about the source of this ability. She said, "Sometimes when I start speaking in my tongue I feel the presence of evil and it makes me feel dirty."

I asked her if the leadership of her church had ever tested the spirit controlling her tongue to see if it was in fact from God. She said she was not aware of any such testing by the leadership in her church for her or anyone else. I said that for us to test the spirit controlling her tongue she would have to agree that it must respond to me in English because I do not have the gift of interpretation. This is possible because the spirit of the prophet is subject to the prophet according to 1 Corinthians 14:31–33. (It is clear from the Apostle Paul's directives on the proper and orderly use of spiritual gifts as outlined in 1 Corinthians 14:26-33 that Christians have the ability and responsibility to exercise particular gifts or not, depending upon the circumstances of the opportunity.) I next told her she would have to agree to renounce this spirit if it would not confess Jesus Christ as come in the flesh. She was frightened but anxious to get to the bottom of her concerns. She said she would be honest and agreed to both ground rules.

I asked her to begin speaking in her tongue. She did so freely. As she was speaking in her tongue I asked, "Spirit of the tongue, will you confess Jesus Christ as come in the flesh?" She continued to speak in her tongue. There was no response to my question. I repeated the same question. This time in the middle of her speaking it broke into English and said, "Maybe, maybe."

I commanded the spirit of the tongue that had responded "maybe" to confess Jesus Christ as come in the flesh. This time it said, "No." Sarah broke into tears at this point. I told the spirit controlling her tongue that it could not be from God because it refused to comply with a test that God has commanded we give to protect the church from deception.

I commanded the spirit to give its name and to explain the work it was doing in Sarah's life. The name it gave was "Selah." It said its work was deception. It indicated its commission was *to divert Sarah's attention from the Giver to the gift*. It wanted her spiritual security and confidence in her "gift" rather than in the giver.

I asked the spirit when it had taken advantage of Sarah. It said, "when she called out for me." I commanded to know when that was, and it said, "when she said Jesus was not enough and she wanted more."

I asked Sarah if she was ready to renounce this spirit and to ask God to forgive her for believing the lie that Jesus had held out on her and that He was not enough, because Scripture clearly says in Romans 8:32, "*Indeed, He who did not spare His own Son, but gave Him up for us all, how will He not also, along with Him, freely give us all things?*" Ephesians 1:3 is just as emphatic, stating, "*Blessed is the God and Father of our Lord Jesus Christ, who has blessed us with every spiritual blessing in the heavenly realms in Christ.*"

A lie from the pit of hell had deceived Sarah. But it was a lie that sounded spiritual and that even her friends encouraged her to believe. Jesus is enough, and anyone denying this is denying God's Word. Sarah prayed for more and got more. But unfortunately, at least in this case, the more she got was not what she thought she was getting.

Sarah asked God to remove this spirit, and He did. She also no longer felt the presence of evil. She was happy but concerned about how her husband, who was a leader in their church, would take this news and how her church would respond to her when they found out her gift was counterfeit.

The next day her husband showed up at my office. His opening remarks surprised me. I was concerned he was going to verbally attack me for interfering with his wife's "blessing." Quite to the contrary, he thanked me for being available to help his wife with something that he knew had been troubling her for some time. I was impressed with his maturity.

What transpired in our conversation and demonic confrontation over the next several hours was the most intriguing and deceptively clever encounter I have had with a demonized Christian in nearly twenty-five years. It was also productive, enlightening and God honoring as we both learned more about demonic deception than either of us had previously understood.

After a few minutes of small talk, he said that in light of his wife's experience he thought it was necessary for him to confirm the validity of his tongue being from God for his sake, and for my sake, because he did not want me to mistakenly think that his wife's experience was normative for all those professing to have the gift of tongues. (I reassured Ben that I had not made that assumption, and his concern in that respect was appreciated, but unnecessary.) Ben assured me that even though his wife's gift had not been from God, he knew his was. He recounted for me how he had received his gift years earlier and told me that he had been an elder at his church for the last twenty years.

I agreed to assist him in testing the source of his tongues-speaking ability after receiving the same assurances from him regarding the two ground rules that I had shared with his wife. As he began to speak freely in his tongue, I asked the spirit controlling his tongue to confess Jesus Christ as come in the flesh. As I continued to ask the question, he continued to speak with no response to my question. I finally said, "In the name of the Lord Jesus Christ, we command you to tell us if you are refusing to confess Jesus Christ as come in the flesh."

The response was immediate and in English. "Karl, you are doing a good work, but you do not have to worry about Ben. He is mine, and his gift is from me." I was startled. Ben was overjoyed, laughed and began smiling.

It suddenly dawned on me that the spirit responding with such flattery had still not answered the question regarding Jesus

Christ having come in the flesh. I reasoned to myself that if this spirit were truly the Holy Spirit, as it later claimed, it would have no problem answering this question. I therefore repeated my question, saying, "You have still not answered the question. Will you confess Jesus Christ as having come in the flesh?"

Looking back on it now, it's easy to see that the compliment was meant to throw both Ben and me off, but God was faithful. When I repeated the question after the apparent compliment and confirmation, the spirit's approach changed significantly. In the middle of Ben's rhythmic tongue an emboldened voice spoke in English saying, "How dare you test me. You are not to test the Lord your God. I have told you he is mine, and his gift is from me."

This time I was frightened, but I said, "If you are truly of the Holy Spirit, you would commend me for standing upon the Word of God, and yet you are attempting to intimidate me. Who are you? And will you confess that Jesus Christ has come in the flesh?"

The response this time was, "I am the Holy Spirit." Ben was beaming once again.

I asked Ben to quit speaking for a moment and to think about what was happening. He was excited and reminded me of the spirit's response that it was the Holy Spirit. I asked him, if this was true, why it was having so much trouble answering the question the Holy Spirit commands in 1 John 4:1–6 that we ask. Ben thought this was no longer necessary because it had already clearly identified itself as God the Holy Spirit.

I was unconvinced for two reasons. First, it still had not answered the basic question about Jesus having come in the flesh. Second—and I had not told Ben this—on a number of occasions I have had demonic spirits say their names were "Jesus" or the "Holy Spirit." Typically, when I qualify the name by saying "you mean the Lord Jesus Christ," they quickly say "No, not that Jesus."

I asked Ben to begin speaking in his tongue again. He thought by this time that it was unnecessary, but he wanted me to feel convinced that his gift was genuine. It would have been fine with me if it was. I wasn't rooting against Ben; I just wanted both of us certain we had complied with Scripture. Remember—this test was at his request, not mine. As Ben spoke in his tongue, I asked a different question. I said, "If you are the Holy Spirit, then you are the author of all known languages. Is that true?"

It responded, "I am the Holy Spirit, and I am the author of all known languages."

I then said, "Quote for me John 1:1–10 in Koine Greek."

It said, "I don't have to."

I replied, "The question is not if you have to, but if you can." I repeated the command again.

This time it said, "I can't."

Ben's smile disappeared in an instant. He said, "Something is wrong. There's no way you could tie the Holy Spirit in a knot like this."

I agreed with him. The work it identified was similar to the answer given by his wife. The work involved deception, and, like Sarah, the purpose it stated was to keep Ben's attention and primary ministry message focused on the gifts of the Spirit rather than on the completed work of Jesus Christ.

If this demon involved with Ben had known how to speak Koine Greek, then this question would have backfired badly on both me and Ben. But the real Holy Spirit was leading our time together, and this particular demon was just as ignorant of Koine Greek as Ben was. The result was that its deceptive claim as the Holy Spirit got exposed as a lie, and God set Ben free from demonic bondage.

The thing that struck me as so interesting about this particular confrontation was the demon's extraordinarily deceptive subtlety. Instead of making a nasty challenge, it complimented me at first. "Karl, you are doing a good work." When that approach didn't stop the process, it attempted to intimidate and condemn me: "How dare you test God." This demon took a name that not only didn't sound evil; it was the name of a member of the triune Godhead.

Warfare can be very obvious at one time and extremely subtle at another. Ben and his wife both struggled with demonic problems. But in Sarah's case, she was broken and fearful that something evil had taken advantage of her. Ben, on the other hand, was spiritually proud and certain the power within him was of God. In both cases, the not-so-subtle message they shared was that Jesus Christ and the salvation He gives as a free gift is not enough for life and godliness. This is a blatant lie that Christ's enemies delight in proclaiming. Christians should know better, regardless of which church they attend.

Demons do not seem to care much about what churches we attend or what theological hobbyhorses we consider sacrosanct. They just try to create opportunities to entice Christians into sin, hoping they can obtain handholds or footholds of control in the process so they can create spiritual confusion and destruction.

So what is the bottom line? My work in this particular aspect of Christian ministry has taught me that demons do not care about our respective church associations. But they are very aware of our relationship with Jesus Christ. Their ultimate purpose is to destroy all of us, and we need to wake up and understand this. Many good Baptists and Pentecostals are going to end up in hell because their commitment was to a religious tradition, a denomination or an institution rather than to our risen Savior, the Lord Jesus Christ. I refuse to let fear motivate me, nor will I willingly sell the leadership of either the charismatic or the non-charismatic churches short. It is past time that we begin to fight strategically together against common enemies who hate us all rather than engage in petty arguments. These arguments ultimately amount to very little when compared to our Savior's command to sacrificially love one another as a testimony to the world of our faith's validity. If our idiosyncrasies are greater than our common bond bought in blood by Jesus Christ, why should a dying world care what we believe?

I am responsible to teach the things I have learned that directly or indirectly impact the charismatic and non-charismatic circles of the Christian body of Christ (2 Timothy 2:2). These include lessons on spiritual warfare. If I don't, I am guilty of being unfaithful to God by allowing the fear of man to replace the fear of God as my motivation for serving Him and writing this particular book. I will not allow myself to fall into that trap.

If I consider selling books and receiving royalty checks more important than the truth contained within the pages of those books, I prostitute God on the altars of expediency and materialism. Allowing dishonest greed to drive a book is a problem whether it involves a gutless writer or a greedy publisher. I am certain I could make the same point if the discussion changed to Christian music. Is the primary issue for publication or production what is Biblically correct or what will sell? The people of God must remember that pleasing God is always more important than attempting to please people at the expense of truth. If I must choose between being politically or religiously correct, and being Biblically correct, I will choose to be Biblically correct and to trust that God will honor this decision regardless of who gets offended. And, frankly, I want to believe that the leadership of those involved will be the first to support me, regardless of their theological affiliations, because they have a Biblical and vested interest in caring for those entrusted to their watch-care. Nobody wants to see deception promoted, even if confronting it puts our pride and tradition on the line.

The Bible is supposed to be our standard and rule of faith, not our feelings, denominational distinctives or petty religious partisanship. Whether charismatic or non-charismatic, we are part of one body if we are born again (Ephesians 4:1–6) and serve the same heavenly Father. If we don't support each other now, regardless of our particular distinctives, what kind of neighbors are we going to be in heaven? And what type of explanation will we give God when He asks us why we spent more time arguing about denominational traditions than sharing the Gospel? Unity in Christ should transcend all of our theological differences if we are truly born-again members of the same family (Ephesians 4:1–6).

My non-charismatic brothers and sisters must remember that there is a difference between forbidding the use of spiritual gifts and qualifying them Biblically. On the other hand, charismatic leaders should be the very first to see the need to test and police activities and spiritual gifts generally associated with their movement according to the standards of the Word of God. To fail to do so on either side of this coin is to risk allowing the abusive extremes of a few to malign the entire Christian movement. Ultimately this will bring disrepute upon everyone claiming Christ as Savior and Lord.

If demonic deception is going to increase as the return of Christ for His church nears, it is imperative that Christian leaders in both charismatic and non-charismatic churches exercise discernment, discipline, power and sound judgment. At a time when the church desperately needs awareness of the subtleties of spiritual warfare we don't need a turf war within the body. From my experience working in this area of ministry, neither charismatic nor non-charismatic believers are immune to demonic deception and attacks on their membership. Christ is bigger than denominational lines, and Christ's love is a stronger bond than the spiritual gifts we exercise and the doctrinal distinctives we teach. First Corinthians 13 certainly makes it clear that our love for each other is more important to God than the specific spiritual gifts we profess to possess.

Another subtlety in spiritual warfare I learned to contend with early in my training was how to respond to demons that purposely attempt to confuse those involved in demonic confrontation by claiming to have the same name as a demon previously confronted. Let me explain.

Remember that when a person confesses sin and cancels ground, demons will leave upon command. They don't like being sent to the pit, but they will go. However, if there are still other demons left who have not been confronted in the demonized individual, these demons will do anything they possibly can to avoid being forced to leave. On several occasions I've had demons respond by giving the same name as a demon previously sent to the pit. The confusing message they are attempting to convey is simple. By giving the same name as a previously deposed associate they hope the demonized individual and the friend standing with them in the fight will assume the demons commanded to leave have either come back or that God didn't have the power to make them leave in the first place. The demonized individual is then supposed to react in fear and shut down the process. The assumption is that since there is apparently no hope in making them leave, what's the use of continuing to fight against them? It's a good plan if you're a condemned demon and your goal is to confuse, play and hide.

When this occurs, what in reality is happening? A demon watches one of its associates get permanently dispatched to a place of torment. Realizing that it's just a matter of time before it heads that way, too, the demon formulates a plan to confuse the parties involved. It hopes to shut down the process because they don't want to leave the one they have a commission to destroy. What to do? How is a demon to continue to confuse, hide, and stay? Idea! Repeat the name of a demon already addressed. Run a calculated bluff to see if the lie so flusters the demonized individual or the person assisting that it undermines, slows down, or shuts down the entire process. The accusatory arrows that will follow are not hard to predict.

> *You didn't have enough faith for this to work. We are more powerful than God. That person helping you doesn't know what he's doing. You'll never get away from us. Stop this now or things are going to get even worse for you.*

The demonized individual is then supposed to panic and run away from the help back into the teeth and claws of the roaring lion who seeks his destruction. After planting the negative thoughts, demons hope the individual will replace sound thinking with fear and doubt.

> *Oh no. This isn't working. I don't have enough faith. The demon(s) were told to leave and they're still there. It's the same name. I thought it had to*

go. I confessed my sin and asked God to cancel the ground held against me, just as I was told to do, but the demon(s) didn't go. Maybe the person helping me doesn't really know what he's doing. Maybe I've committed some sin that God just won't cleanse. Maybe...maybe...maybe...

The first time I ran into this scenario I felt confused for a moment. But God is good and gracious. I commanded the bound demon to declare if it would stand as truth before the white throne of God that the duplicated name it gave was its real name. The response was "No." I commanded in the name of the Lord Jesus Christ that the demon explain why it had lied and taken an associate's name. It explained what is now so obvious. It had hoped that in the confusion of the moment, it could slip away, hide and continue its infernal work. It hoped the demonized individual would react in fear rather than stand by faith and that he would believe a lie that the demon was stronger than the Lord Jesus Christ. It hoped to thus discourage the person from continuing the process.

On a related note, I have discovered that a Christian can bind a demon by any name he or she feels so inclined to name it. If a demon gives a ridiculous name in an attempt to discredit the process or to mock those involved, it is easy to declare: "You have responded to the name _____. We therefore bind you by the name _____, and you will go to the pit bound by that name."

The response is almost predictable. The demon will typically insist that it lied and that the name we just bound it by wasn't its real name and that it doesn't want go to the pit bound with a new name. I remind the demon that it has no say in the matter and that since it chose to play the game it will now have to pay the dues, for eternity.

What about generational sin? I've already offered the answer to this question in a previous chapter. A short reminder to this potentially confusing issue is that we should confess and cancel generational sin like any other sin that has allowed a demon to gain ground or a foothold against a believer. When a person tells me that he is struggling with an issue that has been a consistent problem throughout his family for several generations it isn't difficult to suggest that the source of that particular struggle could be ancestral.

Generational sin doesn't seem fair, but it is real nonetheless. I run into more people struggling with this problem than I used to. I believe part of the answer to this phenomenon is that so many young adults struggling to walk with Christ today have parents who were part of a generation that openly declared God was dead and decided to rebel against organized religion and Christianity in particular. Having burned out on everything other than Christianity, some are slowly responding to the faith they once mocked, but with great difficulty. How many parents who threw caution to the wind realized that they were also setting up their children and children's children for spiritual warfare with demonic spirits?

Demons will respond when they know they must. But they are not anxious to reveal themselves and will hide if given an opportunity. One of the ways they attempt to hide is by a higher ranking demon pushing a subordinate up front when the demon holding higher rank and authority receives a command to come forward. Sometimes lesser ranking demons seem more frightened of higher ranking demons than they are of God. This may seem odd at first glance, but think about it from the perspective of a lower ranking demon. It isn't sure that the Christians who are opposing it really understand much about spiritual warfare in general or deliverance specifically. It also knows that a higher ranking demon can make life intolerable for disobeying orders if the deliverance process breaks down. Do you invite certain wrath from a superior or take a chance and lie, hoping you can avoid leaving by confusing your opponents?

From the higher ranking demon's perspective the risk may be worth taking as well. If the Christians involved in the deliverance understand their delegated authority from Jesus Christ then it is just a matter of time before it is heading to the pit. If, though, it can intimidate a flunky to take its place then maybe it can stay if the Christians involved naively assume that the departing demon represents the sum total of the demonic opposition they are battling. From this demon's point of view what does it have to lose? If it is caught breaking the ground rules then the cost will be painful, but what if it can quietly sneak away undetected? It may think the risk worth the gamble.

It isn't by accident that attacks from both inside and outside the true church of God consistently focus on the inerrancy of the Bible and the true nature of Jesus Christ. It's not coincidental that feelings and personal opinions about religious beliefs often receive more attention than Bible study. When Christians set aside what Scripture clearly says in favor of personal opinions, interpretations, dreams, visions or denominational distinctives, then we have sacrificed the only inerrant, infallible standard for truth given to the church on the altar of personal opinion. Although this may be a popular choice today in some religious circles, it is still dangerous. A neutered view of the Bible is producing a neutered church and spiritually compromised Christians who are more concerned about being viewed politically correct than Biblically correct.

Relativizing Biblical standards is popular in our society. But the true church of God shouldn't be surprised when it becomes evident that religious people raised apart from total dependence upon God and His Word have reproduced godless or spiritually anemic children who pay more attention to the opinion polls, the television and talk show programs than they do to the Word of God. It takes tremendous courage to shine out brightly as stars in the midst of a crooked and perverted world that is lost and groping in darkness. This is particularly true when you know that non-Christians outside the church and compromised Christians inside the church will ostracize you for standing on the rock of God's Word rather than apologizing for it. It is easier to just blend into the chaotic morass that surrounds us in the name of religious tolerance and progressive compassion.

It is past time for Christians who refuse to compromise and marginalize God's Word to wake up, stand up and speak out with conviction and without apology in the public arena.

Pluralism is supposed to work for everyone in our country, not just elitists preaching moral, ethical and religious relativism through their bully pulpits in Hollywood, the K-12 public school system, college degree mills and op-ed columns. Are the champions of tolerance willing to be tolerant of those they label as intolerant? The irony of this duplicity and hypocrisy is that relativism's purveyors demand the very tolerance and freedom they rarely grant to anyone who dares to disagree with their worldview.

If the first century Christians had believed it better to blend into society than to stand up and speak out, we wouldn't be here today possessing and professing faith in Jesus Christ. Christianity would've died in its infancy. If Christians continue to allow a secular society to dictate our views on the realities of spiritual warfare, we will once again allow God's wisdom to become subjugated to the wisdom of man and the deception of demons.

Demonic warfare is a reality, even if many psychologists and medical specialists cannot recognize it or write a prescription for its cure. Counselors routinely remind preachers that we are neither professional counselors nor medical doctors. The not-so-subtle message is that when we get in over our heads we should be willing to refer parishioners to experts trained to provide a specific type of help. This is usually good advice.

It would be refreshing if more medical professionals allowed themselves the freedom to admit their own limitations and heed their own sound advice when they run into issues they aren't trained to address. Sometimes it seems like it's easier to get a Planned Parenthood abortionist to consider teaching a class on abstinence than it is to find medical or counseling professionals who will seriously consider the reality of supernatural entities—whether the discussion focuses upon God or demons. This is the unfortunate current status quo. And it is forcing many sincere individuals to suffer in the silent torment of demonic bondage as they empty their bank accounts and endure the mental taunting that tells them they are beyond hope.

Counselors who profess a belief in Jesus and the Bible while denying the reality and possibility of demonic bondage ought to add a second sign to the one already hanging on their wall of shame. Besides a sign reading, "Payment Demanded in Advance" they need to add, "Medicate and wait."

Shepherds have a responsibility to provide for the needs of the sheep allotted to their care. At times the shepherd may feel uncomfortable doing it, but that shouldn't keep him from doing his job. When we allow wolves, lions and bears to roam at will, it's only a matter of time before the sheep begin to disappear. As spiritual shepherds we have a responsibility to protect the sheep entrusted to our care from predators, both physical and spiritual, regardless of whether we are comfortable doing so or not.

If we choose to do any less we run the risk that the Good Shepherd will identify us as hirelings selfishly motivated by fear to save our own lives rather than courageously protecting the sheep under our care.

> *He who is a hireling, and not a shepherd, who is not*
> *the owner of the sheep, beholds the wolf coming,*
> *and leaves the sheep, and flees, and the wolf*
> *snatches them, and scatters them. He flees because*
> *he is a hireling, and is not concerned about the*
> *sheep.* John 10:12–13

Conclusion: The Challenge

Fight Strategically, Not Just Sincerely

I have said much about this topic of spiritual warfare. My objective for writing this book was to clearly communicate a message and material that a new Christian can understand and that a warrior can use. My desire is that the material be simple, Biblical and transferable. If you read this and walk away in a fog, then I've failed to do my job. If the topic has frightened you rather than encouraged you, then I haven't communicated as clearly as I should have. We are more than conquerors in Christ. It's time we began living like victors in this world rather than as victims. Our Savior and our faith are more than enough to guarantee we have consistent victory over the world, the flesh and the devil— assuming we learn to fight strategically and Biblically with the weapons at our disposal.

Our enemies—the world, the flesh and the devil (sociological, physiological and supernatural opposition)— represent every possible combination of spiritual warfare we will encounter in this life. We must learn how to recognize all three enemies and not focus on one at the expense of the others. In Christ we have the authority and the power to consistently walk above their temptations and propositions if we will learn how to discern the source of our battles and apply the proper defense system God has designed for each enemy.

I will end this book with the same plea I began it with. Christians must know what they believe, why they believe and how to communicate this to others. This must include the subject of spiritual warfare in general and demonic warfare specifically. To do less is disobedience.

One of my spiritual mentors used to tell his classes that we must be diligent in our study to make certain we are not relativizing absolutes or absolutizing relatives. That was good advice more than thirty years ago, and it is still good advice today. There is nothing wrong with writing position papers and challenging people to think. But it is a problem when we allow our personal opinions on Scripture or ecclesiastical loyalties to supersede the Scriptures themselves.

The traditional paradigm of "oppression" and "possession" generally associated with spiritual warfare may be popular, but it is incomplete and therefore inadequate. It leaves too many dedicated but emotionally tormented and mentally paralyzed Christians standing outside the subjectively defined boundaries of this paradigm. It relegates them to living their Christian lives in isolation and in a debilitating sense of hopelessness rather than with the inner joy of freedom in Christ.

A paradigm shift to "oppression" "demonization" and "possession" not only incorporates a more comprehensive understanding of Scripture on the subject of demonic warfare, it also allows for the possibility of resolving demonic problems rather than just attempting to define them.

It is past time for Christians to stand up to the challenge of successfully identifying and confronting the world, the flesh and the devil rather than running from them or ignoring them. If we want to win more battles than we lose we must learn how to consistently fight our opposition Biblically rather than just sincerely. Sincerity is not enough, and ignorance is not bliss.

We are living in the midst of a spiritual war. The victories are real and so are the casualties. In 1 Corinthians 16:13-14 Paul wrote:

Be on the alert, stand firm in the faith, act like men, be strong. Let all that you do be done in love.

Paul's admonition to Christians is just as relevant today as it was then! Christians have been called by God to be soldiers, not spectators.

APPENDICES

Appendix 1

Demonic Warfare:
The Process Overviewed

1. **Meeting One**

   a. Attempt to determine the person's relationship to Christ.

   b. Discuss the importance and priority of a person's will in relation to warfare.

   c. Explain the concept of substitutive thinking— winning in your mind. Challenge the individual to consistently practice this until the "problem" is either under control or he is convinced the issue is greater than memorization and mind renewal. (Check the gas gauge before you overhaul the engine.)

   d. If the habitual accusation continues in spite of consistent application of Scripture and prayer, then make a list using Galatians 5:19–21, Mark 7:21–23 and Colossians. 3:5–8. Detail areas of sin identified in these verses that represent consistent personal problems.

   e. Call and make another appointment. I will not call you.

2. **Meeting Two**

a. Go over the list and group-related issues and concerns.

b. Clearly explain the concepts of confessing and canceling sin.

c. Lay down the ground rules.

d. Verbally affirm the four declarations that are true for all believers in Jesus Christ. (Victory, Colossians 2:13–15; Authority & Protection, Luke 10:18–20; and Position, Ephesians 1:18–2:8.)

e. Determine the two or three most serious concerns to address first.

f. Carefully confess the sin involved in the first area chosen and ask God to cancel all ground given to demons through that particular sin.

g. Address only that spirit holding the highest authority of the group bound and brought forward. Do not waste time with underlings; they will leave with their immediate supervisor.

h. Ask five questions: Name, Source, Work, Habitual Lies and Ground still held, if any.

i. Command the leader to leave, taking his works and effects and all of his associates with their works and effects with him.

j. Have the individual ask the Holy Spirit to fill every place, space or territory the demons have vacated and now use those same areas to the glory of God.

k. Repeat this simple process with each area identified as a problem.

l. When you have addressed all identifiable areas, command to speak to the highest ranking spirit left, other than the Holy Spirit, in case you have overlooked any demon or area.

3. Explain the three priorities of follow up.

a. Keep short accounts.

b. Pray offensively.

c. Consistently read the Scripture.

Five non-negotiables to remember regarding spiritual warfare in general and confronting demonic accusers specifically

1. Your authority to command demons is delegated to you as a believer; it has absolutely nothing to do with your spiritual gifting, denominational affiliation or personality. Luke 10:18–20 is true for all born-again Christians. To put on some façade that success assisting demonized individuals has anything to do with you having some sort of super spirituality is a lie and shouts to any informed person that you either suffer from arrogance or ignorance regarding spiritual warfare.

2. Your attitude towards demons is important to remember. Demons are losers who have been positionally placed beneath the feet of all true Christians. They are not colleagues to fear, revere or respect. Demons should be stepped on, not made a spiritual equal or sparring partner. When you respond to a demon as an equal you embolden it to resist and fight rather than submit to the authority the Lord Jesus Christ has delegated to you. Luke 10:18–20.

3. Your personal involvement in the deliverance process is not nearly as important as the attitude and proactive

involvement of the person who is seeking freedom from demonic bondage. Personal prayer is powerful, but if the demonized person refuses to resist the demons controlling him or to confess the sin(s) that opened the ground, those demons will continue to control him. You can stand with an adult against the powers of darkness, but you cannot stand for an adult against the powers of darkness.

A parent can stand up for a small child. Demons understand that small children are under the authority and care of their parents. They will respond to a parent's prayer for his child as though that prayer was coming from the small child.

4. Always lay down ground rules before you confront demons and ask God the Holy Spirit to enforce them. Demons understand authority and will willingly submit to the highest authority addressing them. If you give them any excuse to think you do not understand your delegated authority over them or that they can do anything other than submit to your delegated authority, you are inviting needless confrontation and confusion.

5. Christians who turn deliverance into a circus side show by allowing shouting and screaming, while combatants square off in a battle of wits and stamina, either do not understand the nature of their authority over demonic spirits or they have purposely turned the moment into an opportunity for self glorification. A Christian not understanding his delegated authority over demons is a shame. A Christian purposely turning demonic conflict into an opportunity for self aggrandizement is a sham. A Christian ignoring demonic conflict because of fear is pitiful. A Christian who sits on the sideline mocking or attacking fellow Christians who are actually in the battle is a coward.

> *For though we walk in the flesh, we do not*
> *war according to the flesh, for the weapons*
> *of our warfare are not of the flesh, but*

divinely powerful for the destruction of fortresses. We are destroying speculations and every lofty thing raised up against the knowledge of God, and we are taking every thought captive to the obedience of Christ... 2 Corinthians 10:3–5

Be on the alert, stand firm in the faith, act like men, be strong. Let all that you do be done in love. 1 Corinthians 16:13–14

Appendix 2

Spiritual Warfare

Seminar Outline: Part one

The battle is on and the battle is real. Unfortunately, most Christians are losing more battles than they are winning. The victories do not have to go to the opposition, but they will continue to until believers learn to fight Biblically.

Who are our enemies?

The World *I John 2:15–17, James 4:4*
The Flesh *Romans 7:15–25, Galatians 5:17*
The Devil *James 4:7–10, I Peter 5:8–9*

How do they primarily attack Christians?

The World The world is an organized system in opposition to and rebellion against God. *I John 2:16* characterizes the world as: the lust of flesh (physical desires), the lust of the eye (beautiful externals), and the boastful pride of life (selfish ambition).

The Flesh The flesh is represented as an old nature, the old man, or the old self within each individual, including Christians, which is in opposition to and rebellion against God. *Galatians 5:19–21, Colossians 3:5–8* and *Mark 7:21–23* partially list areas that the flesh can easily inflame in this battle.

The Devil   According to Jesus and the Bible, the devil is a real enemy who is in opposition to and rebellion against God. His primary attack against Christians seems to be through debilitating accusations. These accusations are usually mental attacks in the mind carried out by demonic spirits who faithfully serve the devil. *Revelation 12:10* mentions this type of opposition. It is possible that the flaming arrows targeted at Christians mentioned in *Ephesians 6:16* could also represent demonic accusation.

The Christian's defense against the world, the flesh and the devil

The World   *I John 2:17* indicates that we are to **evaluate** alluring temptation and say "No." We should not sacrifice the eternal things of God for the temporal things of this world. Christians do not have to pretend that the tinsel and trappings of this world don't sometimes look good. The real issue is whether or not the temporal pleasures of this world are worth the eternal price tag that accompanies them.

The Flesh   *Galatians 5:16* and *Ephesians 5:18* indicate that if we **walk controlled by the Spirit** we will not carry out the desires of the flesh. *Ephesians 4:20–24* and *Romans 12:1–2* state that victory over our old nature or self is possible through consistently **renewing our mind**.

We replace or substitute our old wrong way of thinking with new Christ-like thinking contained in the Bible. Lastly, *II Timothy 2:22* declares that in some situations involving the flesh the faithful believer should simply **run**.

The Devil   Scriptures like *James 4:7–8* and *I Peter 5:8–9* indicate that the Christian is to firmly **resist** the attacks of the devil. Jesus' example in *Matthew 4:1–*

11 shows that He used scripture against the devil when confronting him.

Remember:

A	Accusation or Conviction, B/B, General or Specific
B	Pronouns are Important
C	Offensive Prayer Works
D	You Must Know the Word if You Hope to Use it in Battle

Problem

The world, the flesh and the devil are real opponents who attack Christians in different manners. Since Christians are to defend themselves in diverse manners according to which enemy they are confronting, it becomes extremely important for a Christian to know which enemy he is dealing with so he knows which defense system to activate. If the Christian doesn't know how to correctly identify his enemies as they attack, will he stand firm in his resistance (devil defense), be filled with the Spirit, renew his mind, or run (flesh defense)? Or should he evaluate the situation and say no (world defense)?

Sadly, most Christians do not understand warfare. They do not understand the defense systems at their disposal. Therefore, most Christians lose more battles than they win, and end up blaming God for their failures. The real truth of the matter is that the defense systems will work just as God designed them to. But we must aim them at the right enemy for effectiveness. The real problem isn't with the system; it's with the operator.

The battles are on, and the battles are real. The victories are real, and so are the casualties. Christian, are you winning more battles than you are losing? Do you understand the opposition? Do you understand your defense systems? Are you blaming God for your defeats? Is it time to study God's Word so you can fight your opposition Biblically? Sincerity is not enough.

SPIRITUAL WARFARE

Seminar Outline: Part Two

1   It is time for the traditional paradigm on demonic warfare to shift, even if this change challenges traditional theological opinions and personal comfort levels.

    a)   The Traditional Paradigm: Oppression/Possession

    b)   A Different Paradigm Model that is Consistent with Scripture and Corresponds More Accurately to the Real Life Experience of Many Genuine Christians: Oppression/Demonization/Possession

2   Why is the subject of demonic warfare consistently ignored or mocked even among many justified, sanctified, born-again, baptized, regenerated, saved, church-going, choir-singing, pew-throwing, hooping evangelical Christians?

    a)   Fear
    b)   Ignorance
    c)   Theological Association
    d)   Religious Hucksters

3   The New Testament addresses the issue of demonic warfare in a straightforward, matter-of-fact manner rather than as a novel oddity.

    a.   Ephesians 6:10–18
    b.   Revelation 12:10–12

c.   Ephesians 4:25–27
d.   2 Corinthians 2:10–11
e.   2 Corinthians 11:1–4, 12–15
f.   Matthew 4:1–11
g.   2 Corinthians 10:3–5
h.   Luke 9:49–50
i.   Acts 19:13–20
j.   Luke 10:17–20
k.   Luke 13:10–17
l.   Acts 5:1–5

4   I have heard demons cannot control a Christian
        because the temple of God and the temple of Baal
        have nothing in common. 2 Corinthians 6:14–18

    a. If it's not possible for the temple of God and the
        temple of Baal to have anything in common,
        why is this exhortation necessary?
    b. What do these verses specifically and
        contextually say about Christians being immune
        to demonic attack or control?
    c. Is the temple of the Holy Spirit (our body) still
        the abode for a Christian's flesh or old nature,
        which Paul identifies as an evil member
        dwelling within each believer and in active
        opposition against the Spirit of God? Romans
        7:15–25, Galatians 5:17
    d. If the flesh through habitual sin can still control
        Christians, to whom Christ has given authority
        and victory over the flesh (Galatians 5:16), what
        would compel Christians, who have received
        authority and victory over demonic spirits (Luke
        10:18–20), to believe it is impossible for
        demonic spirits to control them if they willingly
        give up handholds or ground through habitual
        sin (Ephesians 4:27)?

5   How do demons typically attack Christians?

    a. Demonic warfare is usually mental—2 Corinthians 11:1–4

    b. Accusation/Arrows—Revelation 12:10–11, Ephesians 6:16

    c. Divisions, distractions and distortions—take the head, get the body.

    d. Isolation

6   How do demons hold ground or gain handholds against Christians?

    a. Habitual sin: Christians choose to give up a place, a space or a territory of control to an enemy by swimming with leeches. Ephesians 4:25–27

    b. Ancestral sin: The New Testament has nowhere abrogated generational sin.

7   How can Christians discern the difference between the demonic oppression that all believers experience and more severe demonization, which no Christian should ever experience or tolerate?

    a. Demons do not go on vacation.

    b. Arrows can fly, but they should not fill the sky.

    c. Mental paralysis, suicidal depression, irrational fear, a bitter/unforgiving attitude, self-destructive thinking and an overwhelming sense of guilt or false guilt are not from the Holy Spirit of God, but they are all consistent with demonic attacks.

    d. Some things just do not fit, and labels, pills, counseling and memorization do not seem to touch them.

8   Is it possible to be possessed, i.e. completely and
        totally controlled, subjugated and dominated, by
        demons?

        a. Non-Christians—Yes
        b. Christians—No

9   Is it possible to give up specific areas of control to
        demonic spirits?

        a. Non-Christians—Yes
        b. Christians—Yes

10   If ground has been lost to demonic control, can it be
        reclaimed and re-surrendered to Christ? Is it
        possible to break demonic bondage once it has
        occurred?

        a. Non-Christians—Only if they become
            Christians. The person without Christ does not
            have authority to reclaim ground lost through
            demonic control. According to Jesus Christ that
            authority has only been given to Christians
            (Luke 10:18–20). Ultimately, until a person
            becomes a Christian, their Lord and father is
            Satan, whether they realize it or not, religious or
            not (Matthew 12:24–30, John 8:38–47,
            Ephesians 2:1–3).
        b. Christians—Yes—Because all Christians are
            positionally part of the body of Christ, seated far
            above all rule power and authority (Ephesians
            1:18–23, Ephesians 2:4–7) and have been
            delegated authority by Christ over all the
            powers of the enemy (Luke 10:18–20), they do
            not have to remain under demonic control and
            bondage. Since there is no one stronger or
            having more authority than the Lord Jesus
            Christ in heaven or on earth, in this age or any

age to come (Matthew 28:18, Ephesians 1:21)
He is able to bind, subjugate and plunder any
strong man regardless of its power, position, or
authority, natural or supernatural (Matthew 12:
29).

 c. A believer's victory over demonic power is all
about our delegated authority through Christ and
our position in the body of Christ; it has
absolutely nothing to do with spiritual gifting,
human personality, church affiliation or self-
proclaimed faith to name and claim spiritual
healing.

11 How can ground lost to demonic control be
reclaimed and not lost again?

 a. Remember three "C's": Confession, Canceling
and Commanding.
 b. Keep short accounts with sin. Sin can open
doors; confession closes them.
 c. Pray offensively rather than just defensively
(Psalm 35:1–8).
 d. Stay in the Book—If Jesus used the Scriptures
to resist the devil, we are arrogant or naive to
think we can be successful in spiritual warfare
without knowing the Word of God and learning
how to skillfully utilize the sword we have been
given for battle as Christian soldiers of Christ (2
Timothy 2:15; Hebrews 4:12; Ephesians 6:10–
18).

It is time for God's warriors to lock arms and to confront the gates
of hell rather than be trampled underneath them. In Christ we are
more than conquerors. We must live and walk as victors rather
than as victims. I pray this book helps to that end.

About the Author

Karl I. Payne became a Christian June 17th, 1970 through a Young Life ministry in Sacramento, California. He completed his undergraduate degree in Humanities at California State University Sacramento. He attended classes at Multnomah School of the Bible and obtained a Master's of Divinity degree in Pastoral studies and a Doctorate of Ministry degree in Leadership Development at Western Seminary, Portland, Oregon.

By God's grace, Karl credits Joe Simmons (Young Life leader and Philosophy professor), Pat Hurley (Campus Crusade for Christ leader), Josh McDowell (apologist), Dr. Lee Toms (beloved senior pastor) and Dr. Earl Radmacher (seminary president and professor) as the five Christian men God used as mentors or ministry role models to significantly help shape the Christian leader he is today.

Since 1980 Karl has served as the Youth Pastor at Fourth Memorial Church, Spokane, Washington, the College Pastor at Shadow Mountain Community Church, El Cajon, California, and the Pastor of Leadership Development and Discipleship at Antioch Bible Church in Redmond, Washington. He is the President of a registered and tax exempt 501c3 foundation, Transferable Cross Training (TCT), www.karlpayne.org, and has served as the Chaplain for the Seattle Seahawks NFL football team for the last fourteen seasons. He is a popular retreat, conference and seminar speaker and continues to teach classes on discipleship, apologetics and leadership development for a large home school co-op serving the greater Seattle area, Legacy. Karl is also the director of the Worldview/Apologetics Conference that began as an idea in his head in 2002 and has subsequently grown into a large and growing annual conference drawing attendees from the entire Northwest and British Columbia.

Karl has co-authored two books, *A Just Defense*, Multnomah Press, 1987, and *Cross Training*, Multnomah Press, 1993. He has also contributed to two research volumes, *The Encyclopedia of Biblical and Christian Ethics*, edited by R.K. Harrison, Thomas Nelson Publishers, 1987, and *The Popular Encyclopedia of Apologetics*, edited by Ed Hindson and Ergun Caner, Harvest House Publisher, 2008. Karl is the author of a popular three volume discipleship/apologetics series entitled: *Transferable Cross Training: Essentials*, Vol.1, *Transferable Cross Training: Apologetics*, Vol. 2, and *Transferable Cross Training: Leadership*, Vol. 3.

Karl has been married to his bride, Gail, for thirty-two years. They met in their church college group at Arcade Baptist Church in Sacramento, California. They have one son, Jonathan, who is now a twenty-one-year-old college student.

CPSIA information can be obtained
at www.ICGtesting.com
Printed in the USA
LVHW111321270519
619171LV00001B/76/P